中国银行业协会
CHINA BANKING ASSOCIATION

中国银行业
社会责任报告

China Banking Corporate Social Responsibility Report

2017

中国银行业协会　编

中国金融出版社

责任编辑：董　飞

责任校对：李俊英

责任印制：程　颖

图书在版编目(CIP)数据

中国银行业社会责任报告. 2017（Zhongguo Yinhangye Shehui Zeren Baogao）/
中国银行业协会编. — 北京: 中国金融出版社，2018.9

　　ISBN 978-7-5049-9725-8

　　I. ① 中 …　II. ① 中 …　III. ① 银行业—社会责任—研究报告—中国—2017
IV. ① F832

中国版本图书馆CIP数据核字（2018）第201716号

出版

发行　　中国金融出版社

社址　　北京市丰台区益泽路2号

市场开发部　（010）63266347，63805472，63439533 (传真)

网 上 书 店　http://www.chinafph.com

　　　　　　　（010）63286832，63365686 (传真)

读者服务部　（010）66070833，62568380

邮编　　100071

经销　　新华书店

印刷　　北京市松源印刷有限公司

尺寸　　210毫米×285毫米

印张　　6

字数　　200千

版次　　2018年9月第1版

印次　　2018年9月第1次印刷

定价　　78.00元

ISBN 978-7-5049-9725-8

如出现印装错误本社负责调换　联系电话(010) 63263947

序言一

2017 年是举世瞩目、意义非凡的一年，党的十九大、第五次全国金融工作会议、中央经济工作会议等重要会议召开，为中国银行业指明发展方向、提供根本遵循。中国银行业金融机构深入贯彻党中央、国务院的各项决策部署，以供给侧结构性改革为主线，围绕服务实体经济、防控金融风险、深化金融改革三大任务，不断创新，提供强有力的金融支持，在新时代全面助力中国经济实现由高速增长向高质量发展的转变。

深化供给侧结构性改革。 2017 年，中国银行业金融机构持续推动落实"三去一降一补"五大任务，深化改革，积极创新。实施精细化的行业信贷政策，深入开展市场化法治化债转股，落实住房贷款差异化投向政策，加强服务收费管理和增加金融供给，加大对经济社会发展薄弱环节支持力度等，有效提升金融资源配置效率，提高防范和化解金融风险的能力，助推我国产业结构调整和经济转型升级。

助力创新驱动。 2017 年，中国银行业金融机构聚焦制造业发展的难点痛点，创新符合行业特点的信贷管理体制和金融产品，支持高端装备、新一代人工智能、"互联网 +"应用等先进制造业和科技领域的资金需求，有效促进新旧动能接续转换。

坚持精准扶贫。 2017 年，中国银行业金融机构坚持服务国家精准扶贫、精准脱贫的战略，聚焦"三区三州"等深度贫困地区，因地制宜创新扶贫授信服务和融资模式，扩大扶贫小额信贷覆盖面，精准满足建档立卡贫困户生产、创业、就业、搬迁安置等各类金融需求，培育贫困地区"造血"功能，助力实现到 2020 年打赢脱贫攻坚战、全面建成小康社会的目标。截至 2017 年底，银行业金融机构发放扶贫小额信贷余额为 2 496.96 亿元，支持建档立卡贫困户 607.44 万户，贫困县行政村基础金融服务覆盖率达 95.83%，较年初提高 2.93 个百分点。

支持"三农"发展。 2017 年，中国银行业金融机构以实施乡村振兴战略为"三农"金融服务工作总抓手，聚焦农户、新型农业经营主体，加大信贷投放，创新特色产品，支持农业生产、农村基础设施建设、返乡下乡人员就业创业，不断扩大基础金融服务覆盖面，打通服务"三农"的"最后一公里"。截至 2017 年底，银行业涉农贷款余额 30.95 万亿元，同比增长 9.64%，其中农户贷款余额 8.11 万亿元，同比增长 14.41%，全年实现涉农贷款持续增长目标。

服务对外开放。 2017 年，中国银行业金融机构积极适应对外开放新形势，统筹推进服务"一带一路"顶层规划，通过优化多双边合作、完善全球网络、深化自贸区建设、创新产品组合、打造境内外融资和支付结算平台等多元化金融措施，促进企业和产业"走出去""引进来"，推动多项重大海外项目落地，持续加快人民币国际化进程。截至 2017 年底，共有 10 家中资银行在 26 个"一带一路"沿线国家设立了 68 家一级机构；外资银行在华营业性机构总数达 1 013 家，总资产为 3.24 万亿元人民币。

优化客户服务。 2017 年，中国银行业金融机构秉承"以客为尊"的服务理念，密切关注经济金融资源和客户金融需求变化。以"普惠、跨界、安全、效率"为主题，持续加强先进科技手段和管理方式在金融领域的推广应用，优化传统网点，加强电子银行、社区银行、智能银行建设和无障碍服务，开展金融知识普及活动，切实维护消费者权益，构建和谐健康的金融消费环境。截至 2017 年底，银行营业网点总数达到 22.87 万个，新增设营业网点 800 多个。据不完全统计，银行业平均离柜业务率为 87.58%。

完善绿色金融。 2017 年，中国银行业金融机构积极践行"绿水青山就是金山银山"的发展理念，丰富绿色信贷产品、创新绿色金融债券，加大对节能环保领域的资金支持，开展绿色办公运营、传播绿色发展理念，构建银行绿色文化，助力打赢蓝天保卫战，推动生态环境保护、低碳经济发展和美丽中国建设。截至 2017 年 6 月末，21 家主要银行业金融机构绿色信贷余额为 8.22 万亿元，其中，节能环保、新能源、新能源汽车等战略新兴产业贷款余额为 1.69 万亿元，节能环保项目和服务贷款余额 6.53 万亿元。

关注员工发展。 2017 年，中国银行业金融机构强化员工权益保障，重视人才培养，开展全方位、多层次的职业能力培训，举办多彩文体活动，加强困难员工关爱，提升职业幸福感，打造尊重、多元、和谐的工作氛围。据不完全统计，截至 2017 年底，银行业金融机构组织开展员工培训项目逾 32.87 万个，培训项目覆盖 3 037.30 万人次，同比增加近337.90 万人次。

投身公益事业。 2017 年，中国银行业金融机构积极宣传公益责任理念、弘扬公益精神、树立社会责任意识，扩展志愿服务领域，制定社会志愿者行动计划，带动公众营造友善、文明、共享的责任生态，为促进社会和谐打下坚实基础。据不完全统计，截至 2017 年底，公益慈善投入总额达 10.36 亿元，公益慈善项目达 3 307 个；员工志愿者活动时长95.83 万小时。

当前，中国银行业金融机构以习近平新时代中国特色社会主义思想为指导，坚决落实新发展理念，服务国家战略，履行社会责任，助力打好"防控重大风险、精准脱贫、污染防治"三大攻坚战，加大普惠金融、绿色金融的发展，扩大对外开放的广度和深度，提高发展的质量和效益。中国银行业协会将一如既往围绕银行业共同利益的宗旨，发挥"自律、维权、协调、服务"职能，引领银行业金融机构持续提升创新，优化金融供给，共同推进银行业高质量可持续发展，更好地满足人民日益增长的美好生活需要。

是为序！

中国银行业协会会长　田国立

2018 年 6 月

序言二

2017 年，党的十九大、第五次全国金融工作会议、中央经济工作会议等重要会议的召开，为我国金融工作指明了发展方向，提供了根本遵循。中国银行业面对复杂多变的国内外经济金融形势，不忘初心，砥砺前行，谱写了新时代、新征程中履行社会责任的新篇章。2017 年是中银协连续第十年发布《报告》，并且同时发布中英文版本，持续引领会员单位将社会责任理念根植于企业文化，付诸于日常经营管理。本年度《报告》内容全面，案例丰富，总结了过去一年全行业履行社会责任方面的实践思路和具体成果。《报告》主体内容要点如下：

一、银行业稳健运行，促进经济高质量发展

银行是金融稳定的"压舱石"，银行稳则金融稳，金融稳则经济稳。2017 年，在监管部门的有效引领下，银行业运行稳健，银行资产负债结构日趋健康，支持实体经济力度进一步增强，风险抵补能力和流动性储备充足，应对风险的能力进一步增强。截至 2017 年底，我国银行业金融机构本外币资产 252 万亿元，同比增长 8.7%，增速较 2016 年下降 7.1 个百分点；总负债 233 万亿元，同比增长 8.4%，增速较 2016 年下降 8.2 个百分点。银行表外资金逐步回归表内。2017 年，表外业务总规模增速逐月回落，总体呈现收缩态势。在银行业总资产增长 8.7% 的情况下，全年新增贷款 12.6%，相当于在向实体经济多投入信贷资金的同时少扩张资产规模约 16 万亿元。脱实向虚势头得到初步遏制。2017 年，商业银行同业资产负债自 2010 年来首次收缩，同业理财比年初净减少 3.4 万亿元。银行理财因增速下降而少增 5 万多亿元，通过"特定目的载体"投资少增约 10 万亿元。

各项指标稳健。2017 年末，商业银行资产利润率（ROA）为 0.92%，资本利润率（ROE）为 12.56%；资本充足率（CAR）为 13.65%，较上年末上升 0.37 个百分点；拨备覆盖率为 181.42%，较上年末上升 5.02 个百分点；商业银行流动性比例为 50%，银行抵御风险的能力持续提高；不良贷款余额为 1.71 万亿元，不良贷款率为 1.74%，连续四个季度稳定在 1.74% 的水平。

二、助力深化供给侧结构性改革，提升金融服务实体经济的水平和效率

为实体经济服务是银行业的天职和宗旨。2017 年，银行业金融机构紧紧围绕服务实体经济这一重点任务，对实体经济发放的人民币贷款余额为 119.03 万亿元，同比增长 13.2%，为实体经济健康发展提供资金支持。

银行业通过提升精细化管理水平和落实国家产业政策有机结合，实施差异化、精细化的行业信贷政策，大力压缩对产能过剩行业贷款，有序退出"僵尸企业"，坚定不移地推进去产能。通过面向发展前景良好但暂时遇到困难的优质企业开展市场化债转股，积极稳妥推进去杠杆。通过落实差别化住房信贷政策，坚决抑制部分地区的房地产市场泡沫，配合房地产去库存。2017 年，银行业保障性安居工程贷款同比增长 42.3%。通过加强服务收费管理和增加金融供给并举，有效降低成本，2017 年银行业新增减费让利 440 亿元。通过健全普惠金融组织机制，加大对小微、"三农"、扶贫等薄弱领域的金融支持，不断深化科技金融创新，加大对新技术、新产品、新业态、新模式"四新"经济的支持，2017 年，银行业重点推进补短板项目 70 多项。

三、精准扶贫脱贫，助力打赢脱贫攻坚战

银行业金融机构作为扶贫重要力量，始终以"精准扶贫，精准脱贫"基本方略为指导，进一步完善扶贫工作机制，充分发挥开发性、政策性、商业性和合作性金融的多元化优势和互补作用，深入实施东西部扶贫协作，聚焦"三区三州"等深度贫困地区，因地制宜创新扶贫授信服务和融资模式，注重提升脱贫内生发展动力，培育贫困地区"造血"功能，为实现到2020年打赢脱贫攻坚战、全面建成小康社会目标提供有力有效的金融支撑。截至2017年末，银行业金融机构发放扶贫小额信贷余额2 496.96亿元，较年初增长50.58%；支持建档立卡贫困户607.44万户，建档立卡贫困户覆盖率达25.81%，较年初增加8.09个百分点；贫困县行政村基础金融服务覆盖率达95.83%，较年初提高2.93个百分点。2017年，帮扶21万余贫困人口创业脱贫，为贫困户发放扶贫贷款、提供创业贷款金额累计达到111亿元。

四、践行普惠金融理念，不断提高广大人民群众对金融服务的获得感和满意度

大力发展普惠金融，是我国全面建成小康社会的必然要求。2017年，银行业金融机构将践行普惠金融与自身转型发展相结合，积极探索商业可持续性，打造普惠金融产品服务体系，加强金融基础设施建设，提升科技运用水平，搭建互联网金融服务平台，聚焦服务"三农"、小微企业及"大众创业、万众创新"等重点领域，提升特殊群体客户金融服务体验，满足残疾人客户需求，实现构建广覆盖、多层次的供给体系。截至2017年末，银行业涉农贷款余额30.95万亿元，同比增长9.64%，其中农户贷款余额8.11万亿元，同比增长14.41%。小微企业贷款余额30.74万亿元，同比增长15.14%，比各项贷款平均增速高2.67个百分点；小微企业贷款余额户数1 520.92万户，同比增长159.82万户；申贷获得率95.27%，同比上升1.67个百分点，自2015年以来，连续三年实现了小微企业贷款增速、户数、申贷获得率"三个不低于"目标。2017年，累计为137万余名农村青年建立电子信用档案，向超过22万名创业青年提供信贷支持，发放青年创业小额贷款177亿元。

特别是在2017年，为全面提升银行业无障碍服务水平，推动我国银行业无障碍环境建设工作向制度化、规范化、标准化的纵深发展，在中国残疾人联合会吕世明副主席的大力支持下，在多位国家级无障碍环境建设专家的指导下，中银协组织完成了《银行无障碍环境建设标准》制定工作，规范和引导全行业金融机构更好地满足残疾人客户日益增长的金融服务需求。无障碍环境建设是一项系统工程，需要全社会各行业长期共同努力，银行业率先出台首个行业性无障碍环境标准，对提升残疾人公平享受优质高效金融服务水平具有重要意义。

五、积极发挥金融科技作用，不断改进消费者体验和服务效率

银行业以科技创新为驱动力，以"普惠、跨界、安全、效率"为主题，持续加强先进科技手段和管理方式在金融领域的推广应用，升级传统银行服务渠道，不断创新网上银行、电话银行、手机银行、微信银行等电子渠道功能，为客户带来了全天候便捷服务体验。截至2017年底，营业网点总数达22.87万个，全国布局建设自助银行16.84万家，布放自助设备超过80万台，其中创新自助设备11.39万台，客户金融服务获得感持续提升，体验日益优化。2017年，银行业金融机构离柜交易达2 600亿笔，同比增长46.33%；离柜交易金额达2 010亿元，同比增长32.06%；行业平均离柜业务率达87.58%。

银行业金融机构始终秉承"以客为尊"的核心理念，将消费者的放心满意作为服务的标准，持续通过多种形式、多种渠道开展金融知识宣传服务活动，增强银行消费者的自我保护意识和风险责任意识，拉近银行与消费者的距离，赢得消费者的信赖。2017 年，普及金融知识万里行活动共组织近 26 万场次金融知识普及活动，参与银行网点近 16 万个，受众消费者近 3 亿人。据统计，2017 年银行业客服中心人工电话接听量超过 10 亿通；人工电话接通率达到 91%，连续五年高于 90%；自助语音客户满意度达到 98.4%，连续四年保持在 98% 以上。

六、把握机遇，主动适应扩大对外开放新形势

自 2017 年全国金融工作会议作出积极稳妥扩大金融业对外开放，助推金融业做大做强的重要部署以来，国家层面推动金融业扩大开放的措施密集出台。2017 年 8 月，国务院印发《关于促进外资增长若干措施的通知》，从五个方面提出促进外资增长的 22 条政策措施。人民银行、银保监会也相继发布政策，加快推进银行业对外开放。这些开放举措明确了外资银行"国民待遇 + 负面清单"的管理原则，为外资银行在华发展创造了更好的投资和经营环境。截至 2017 年底，外资银行在华营业性机构总数达 1 013 家，近 15 年增长近 5 倍，年均增速 13%，形成了具有一定覆盖面和市场深度的总行、分行、支行服务网络。2017 年底总资产 3.2 万亿元人民币，较 2001 年中国加入世贸组织时增长 10 倍多。2017 年实现净利润相当于 2002 年的 10 倍，注册资本也比 2002 年末增长了 6 倍多。截至 2017 年末，在华外资银行不良贷款率仅为 0.7%，远低于其他各类金融机构，资本充足率 17.83%，拨备覆盖率高达 296.88%，表现出了良好的风险控制能力和经营理念。

银行业从优化海外布局、促进创新发展、强化金融合作等方面服务"一带一路"建设。截至 2017 年末，共有 10 家中资银行在 26 个"一带一路"沿线国家设立了 68 家一级机构，其中包含 17 家子行、40 家分行、10 家代表处、1 家合资银行。在中资机构"走出去"的同时，"一带一路"沿线国家和地区的银行机构也在不断进入中国市场。截至 2017 年末，"一带一路"沿线的 21 个国家的 55 家银行在华设立了 7 家外资法人银行、19 家外国银行分行以及 38 家外国银行代表处。

七、推进绿色发展，共建美丽中国

绿水青山就是金山银山。银行业金融机构响应国家政策，支持环境改善、应对气候变化和资源节约高效利用的经济活动，加大绿色信贷投入，开展绿色办公运营，践行绿色公益环保，致力推动绿色、低碳经济发展和美丽中国建设。2017 年，中银协制定完成《中国银行业绿色银行评价实施方案（试行）》，组织签署《中国对外投资环境管理风险倡议》，编写全球第一本《绿色信贷》（中英文版）教材。银行业金融机构不断完善绿色金融制度建设，合理配置信贷资源，积极参与国际合作，大力支持林业、清洁能源、建筑节能等行业发展。不断创新绿色金融产品服务，加大绿色金融投入，在资金使用、绩效管理、风险控制等方面实施差异化政策，支持企业节能减排，限制"两高一剩"行业发展。截至 2017 年 6 月末，国内 21 家主要银行绿色信贷余额 8.2 万亿元，较年初增长 7.1%；节能环保、新能源、新能源汽车等战略性新兴产业贷款余额为 1.69 万亿元，节能、环保项目和服务贷款余额为 6.53 万亿元。

八、投身公益事业，不忘初心反哺社会

银行业秉承"责任银行 和谐发展"的社会责任理念，深入推进各项公益慈善事业。银行业金融机构持续完善公益管理体系，积极推进社会公益项目建设，促进客户以多元化方式参与公益项目。2017年，银行业金融机构公益慈善投入总额达 10.36 亿元；员工志愿者活动时长 95.83 万小时。截至 2017 年底，公益慈善项目达 3 307 个。

十年风雨兼程，十年耕耘收获。通过银行业金融机构的共同努力，银行业社会责任管理和实践在"质"与"量"上实现了大跨越，成绩斐然。放眼未来，任重道远。2018 年是全面贯彻落实党的十九大精神的开局之年，是决胜全面建成小康社会的关键一年。新时代，银行业要不忘初心，牢记责任使命，探索责任新路径，共同书写银行业社会责任管理工作新篇章，为我国经济实现高质量发展、社会和谐稳定贡献力量！

中国银行业协会党委书记、专职副会长 潘光伟

2018 年 6 月

报告说明

报告时间 2017 年 1 月 1 日至 12 月 31 日

报告周期 年度报告

报告发布情况 2009 年首次发布报告，至今连续第 10 年发布

编制依据

国际标准化组织《ISO 26000：社会责任指南（2010）》

国家标准 GB/T 36000—2015《社会责任指南》

全球报告倡议组织《可持续发展报告指南（G4）》

中国银监会《关于加强银行业金融机构社会责任的意见》

中国银行业协会《中国银行业金融机构企业社会责任指引》

报告范围

本报告涵盖国家开发银行、政策性银行、大型商业银行、邮政储蓄银行、股份制银行、城市商业银行、资产管理公司、农村商业银行、农村信用社、村镇银行、外资银行等 102 家机构提供的内容。

数据说明

中国人民银行、中国银行保险监督管理委员会及会员机构。

报告发布形式

报告以印刷版（案例集以网络版：http://www.china-cba.net/list.php?fid=255）发布

报告以中、英文两种文字发布，两种文本理解上发生歧义时，请以中文文本为准

印刷用纸 环保纸张

编制单位 中国银行业协会

Time Scope From January 1, 2017 to December 31, 2017

Frequency of Publication Annual report

Information about the Report 2018 is the tenth successive year of publication from 2009

Compilation Guideline

ISO 26000 Guidance on Social Responsibility from International Organization for Standardization

GB/T 36000—2015, Guidelines on Social Responsibility

Global Reporting Initiative's Sustainability Reporting Guidelines (G4)

China Banking Regulatory commission's "Opinion on Strengthening Corporate Social Responsibility of Banking Financial Institutions"

China Banking Association's "Guidelines on Corporate Social Responsibility for China's Banking Financial Institutions"

Entities covered

102 institutions involving China Development Bank, policy banks, large commercial banks, Postal Savings Bank of China, joint-stock banks, city commercial banks, asset management companies, rural commercial banks, rural credit cooperatives, village banks, foreign banks.

Source of Data

The People's Bank of China, China Banking and Insurance Regulatory Commission, and member institutions.

Form of Publication

Report in printed version and Case Collection in electronic version: http://www.china-cba.net/list.php?fid=255

The report is published in both Chinese version and English version. Please refer to Chinese version while the content of two versions differs.

Printing Paper Recycled paper

Compilation Organization China Banking Association

目 录

CONTENTS

脚踏实地 践行责任理念

"为贯彻落实党和国家的相关政策要求，响应社会公众对银行业的新期待，银行业要在三方面用心、走心、上心，齐心协力担当好社会责任。一是回归服务实体经济的'初心'，二是赢得社会公众广泛信赖的'信心'，三是追求锤炼责任管理的'匠心'。"

——中国银行业协会党委书记、专职副会长 潘光伟

"银行业金融机构要突出主业，防止脱实向虚，增强服务实体经济能力；要下沉重心，大力发展普惠金融，稳步扩大基础金融覆盖面；要深化责任理念，持续提升履责能力；要强化行业自律，积极推广银行业责任理念与责任文化。"

——中国银保监会宣传工作部主任 梅志翔

"面对新形势，银行业金融机构要重点支持国家战略，满足国家重点领域金融服务需求；要推进'负责任'的金融发展，促进经济社会健康可持续发展；要注重塑造责任品牌，实现自身强劲可持续发展。"

——中国银行业协会第七届会长单位代表、中国银行副行长 张青松

"社会责任工作是个永恒的课题，应怀揣情怀、尽己所能，完成当代人的使命，力求担当作为、问心无愧，各银行业金融机构以及相关机构部门应不断探索，踏实肯做，按照监管要求以及行业标准，从体制、机制建立到人力、财力及物力的配置，不断努力，力求从我做起、点滴进步，立足行业实际，持续加强和健全完善的社会责任管理工作体系，适应新时代要求；坚持创新驱动，不断丰富社会责任管理方式，助力国家战略发展，提升企业可持续发展能力。"

——中国银行业协会秘书长 黄润中

2017年，银行业金融机构深入落实"强监管"要求，脚踏实地践行责任理念，扎实服务实体经济发展。坚决贯彻底线思维，牢牢守住"不发生系统性金融风险的底线"；坚守本源，专注主业，积极服务供给侧结构性改革；主动创新，强化风险防范意识，深化同业合作，大力支持国家对外开放发展；务实求新，聚焦难点痛点，切实提高金融服务专业化、精细化水平，落实制造强国战略。进一步发挥普惠金融、绿色金融在消除贫困、农业可持续、环境保护等领域的关键作用。

深化利益相关方参与机制。银行业金融机构深入推进多方合作，在助力"一带一路"建设、推动产业转型升级、提升"三农"金融服务、扶持小微企业发展、推进绿色发展等领域，通过发挥各方优势，优化各方风险边界，在实现经济效益的同时，兼顾社会与环境效益，致力于推动经济、社会、环境协调可持续发展。

强化责任沟通与交流。银行业金融机构深化与国际国内同业交流，参与联合国全球契约、联合国环境规划署、全球报告倡议（GRI）、赤道原则等社会责任领域相关活动，分享与交流责任管理与实践经验，了解社会责任发展最新趋势。与此同时，在加大业务合作、业务推动过程中，强化责任共识、可持续竞争力等理念的分享，不断营造银行业健康持续发展的良好生态环境。

推动社会责任工作纵深发展。2017年，中国银行业社会责任工作研讨会于北京召开。围绕"夯实责任共识，助力银行业可持续发展"的主题，业内外社会责任管理专家进行了经验分享。经验分享涉及社会责任管理体系设计与责任管理推进，基于可持续发展战略推动可持续发展管理，应对环境挑战与社会需求的产品与服务创新，基于责任理念、责任方法融入的社会责任根植项目四个主题。社会责任研讨会成为银行业分享交流社会责任管理推进平台，并逐步固化为年度性会议，为深化会员银行责任共识、提升行业美誉度，增进社会公众对银行业的信任、构建银行业可持续发展的良好社会生态奠定基础。

2017年是中国银行业协会连续第十年发布中国银行业社会责任报告。《报告》以构建银行业履责长效推进机制、提升银行业履责管理实践水平为根本目标，为行业提供社会责任展示交流平台、管理实践研究平台和绩效检验评价平台，凝聚行业共识，激发内在动力，展示责任形象，不断提升行业责任影响力。

守住底线　防控金融风险

银行业金融机构深入贯彻落实中央经济工作会议"把防控金融风险放到更加重要的位置"的总体要求，按照回归本源、专注主业、下沉重心的原则，以服务国家战略、维护国有资产安全为主线，确立科学的发展理念和战略方向，持续强化合规风险管理，加强决策、执行、监督、评价等治理机制建设，突出重点领域风险化解，多措并举提升风险管控实效，牢牢守住"不发生系统性金融风险的底线"。

银行业金融机构切实增强同风险赛跑、努力跑在风险前面的意识，突出市场风险、信用风险、利率风险、声誉风险、操作风险、科技风险等重点领域风险管控，立足全流程、全方位、全业务加强风险管理，开展实施各类审计、调查及评价，提高风险监测预警及重点领域风控精准度，健全纵向到底、横向到边的全面风险管理责任体系，为各项业务持续稳健发展保驾护航。

银行业金融机构本着"风险为本、合规为先"的原则，积极有效管控洗钱及恐怖融资风险，通过完善系统处理流程、创新洗钱风险监测、甄别、报告处理工作模式等措施，有序开展反洗钱工作；坚持不懈贯彻中央八项规定精神，创新监督机制，全面履行监督职责，完善作风文化建设，扎实推进反腐倡廉；强化人员职业操守和法制观念教育，进一步提高员工的辨别能力、自控能力和醒悟能力。银行业金融机构不断优化内部控制环境，完善内部控制体系，营造良好的合规文化，强化合规风险监测分析，为银行业的稳健运营提供坚实保障。

▶ 银行业在行动

国家开发银行将巴塞尔协议理念和方法融入风险管理实践中，不断深化信用风险内部评级体系建设，建立健全市场风险内部模型法管理体系和操作风险管理体系，强化经济资本在绩效考核、组合管理的应用，形成了独具特色、富有成效的全面风险管理体系和中长期信贷风险管理方法，为业务稳健发展提供了有力保障。

中国农业发展银行加强沟通交流，充分掌握全面风险管理工作的难点和重点问题，围绕资本管理、全面风险管理、RWA 系统建设等内容开展专题研讨，分析全面风险管理体系建设咨询服务需求；积极与外部咨询机构开展合作，正式成立咨询项目组，着手对现有的管理体系进行梳理，形成差异分析报告和改进方案。

中国农业银行优化反洗钱组织架构，在总行和一级分行设立反洗钱中心，集中上收反洗钱监测分析业务；制定大额交易和可疑交易报告管理办法、涉及恐怖活动资产冻结管理办法等专项制度，进一步完善反洗钱制度体系。

中国银行"新一代网络金融事中风控系统"正式上线。新一代系统基于该行互联网金融整体风控体系，全面引入互联网公司在大数据、云计算、机器学习等方面的领先技术，以事中监控为核心，在用户享受便捷互联网金融服务的同时，为其提供全方位、全流程、实时高效的反欺诈服务，切实保障用户资金和账户安全，实现风险防控和客户体验"双提升"。

华夏银行完善工作运行机制，升级反洗钱信息系统，强化高风险业务管控，全面提高反洗钱管理质效。2017 年，该行上线新一代反洗钱系统，成为按照中国人民银行令（2016）第 3 号文件要求报送反洗钱数据的股份制商业银行。全年积极配合监管部门、有权机关开展协查、布控等工作 50 余次。

兴业银行强化风险合规管理，认真落实"三违反""三套利""四不当"专项治理及"市场乱象"整治工作要求，主动在全集团开展"地毯式"风险排查，坚持边查边改、立查立改，有效堵塞漏洞、防范风险。开展"兴航程"合规内控提升年活动，举办"兴风向"综合赛训项目，员工风险意识不断增强。

北京银行建立风险报告机制，定期召开投资机构风险汇报会，及时充分掌握附属机构风险防控情况；建立检查、通报、整改、督导机制，通过检查整改，推动附属机构风险管理工作不断规范完善。

恒生银行（中国）上线新反洗钱交易监测系统，同时，在综合考虑业务特点及客户群体特征、交易习惯等因素的前提下，结合可疑监测模型所需数据与行内核心系统数据抓取的可行性，停止使用原 18 条可疑交易监测规则，形成该行与本地自主监测模型相结合的体系。

一. 牢记使命
服务实体经济

银行业金融机构紧紧围绕服务实体经济、防控金融风险、深化金融改革重点任务，坚守本源，专注主业，主动服务供给侧结构性改革，落实"一带一路"建设、京津冀协同发展、长江经济带等区域战略；深化金融改革，提升综合金融服务能力，助力对外开放发展；围绕"中国制造2025"，着力加强对制造业的转型升级支持力度，不断提升服务实体经济质效，推动实体经济高质量发展。

2017 年[①]

社会融资规模存量为

174.71 万亿元

同比增长 **12%**

其中，对实体经济发放人民币贷款余额为

119.03 万亿元

同比增长 **13.2%**

① 数据来源：中国人民银行。

（一）服务供给侧结构性改革

　　银行业金融机构紧扣供给侧结构性改革，围绕"三去一降一补"五大任务，深化改革，积极创新，继续助推"僵尸企业"优化升级，坚定不移地推进去产能；深入开展市场化法治化债转股，积极稳妥推进去杠杆；落实差别化住房信贷政策，坚决抑制部分地区的房地产市场泡沫，配合房地产去库存；加强服务收费管理和增加金融供给并举，有效降低企业成本；进一步加强对"三农"、小微等薄弱环节和各类新业态新动能领域服务，积极支持"一带一路"建设，为企业"走出去"与"引进来"提供更有效的金融服务。银行业金融机构大力推动绿色金融体系建设，完善绿色金融产品与服务，强化社会与环境风险管理，促进经济社会、环境、协调持续发展。

▶ 银行业在行动

支持去产能

　　国家开发银行、中国工商银行、交通银行等大型商业银行严格落实国家产业政策和"去产能"政策要求，有扶有控，做好金融服务支撑，实施差异化、精细化的行业信贷政策，针对钢铁、煤炭和造纸等产能过剩行业，逐户制定工作推进方案；同时，大力支持先进设备制造业和高新技术产业，助力新产业、新业态和新模式等新经济，支持培育新的经济增长点、形成新动能，促进经济转型升级。

　　2017 年，**国家开发银行**过剩产能行业贷款余额较年初减少 **662** 亿元；**中国农业银行**对钢铁、煤炭等 **13** 个产能过剩和高风险行业压降用信 **1 814** 亿元；**中国建设银行**产能过剩行业贷款余额比上年下降 **79.16** 亿元；**交通银行**产能严重过剩行业贷款余额占比较年初下降 **0.7** 个百分点。

支持去杠杆

　　2017 年 9 月，**中国工商银行**全资子公司工银金融资产投资有限公司开业，致力于帮助企业降低杠杆率，促进企业降本增效、深化改革，为企业量身打造增强资本实力和治理效率的债转股方案。

　　中国建设银行保持市场化债转股先发优势，债转股签约金额 **5 897** 亿元，落地金额 **1 008** 亿元，助力企业降低杠杆水平。

　　交通银行设计债转股相关业务模式和服务方案，引导各级经营单位采取多种方式扎实服务企业"去杠杆"需求。截至 2017 年底，已签署市场化债转股框架协议的项目 **11** 个，框架协议金额 **1 200** 亿元。

　　兴业银行充分考虑不同类型行业和企业的杠杆特征，通过债务融资工具、股权质押融资、产业引导基金等多种直接融资方式，推动非金融企业加大直接融资比重，并积极关注、审慎推进债转股试点，有效帮助企业去杠杆。

支持去库存

　　国家开发银行围绕供给侧结构性改革中心任务，因城施策，积极发放棚改货币化安置贷款；继续发挥棚改融资主渠道作用，全力支持全国棚改建设，积极推动住房租赁试点。截至 2017 年底，该行累计发放棚户区改造贷款 **34 075** 亿元，本年发放棚户区改造贷款 **8 800** 亿元，累计惠及棚户区居民超过 **2 000** 万户。

　　中国农业银行落实国家加快建立租购并举住房制度的相关要求，积极支持人口净流入大中城市的租赁性住房业务发展。

　　中国建设银行积极助推国家"租购并举"政策落地，住房租赁综合解决方案率先在国家住房租赁试点城市广东佛山、深圳落地。

支持降成本

　　浙商银行持续推进池化融资业务迭代创新，通过"池化融资""易企银"以及"应收款链"三大平台为实体经济提供综合性金融服务方案，盘活企业流动资产，助力降成本、增效能。截至 2017 年底，"涌金"系列池化产品为客户累计节省利息支出达 **16.94** 亿元。

　　青岛银行通过银行业债权人委员会运作机制，采取降低贷款利率、减免欠息、调整还款期限和还息频率等方式，有效帮助暂时遇到困难的企业实现产业转型升级，降低融资成本。

国家开发银行积极落实服务"一带一路"建设、京津冀协同发展特别是雄安新区建设等区域发展战略，持续加大支持扶贫、保障性住房、科技创新、生态环保、教育医疗等领域金融资源配置力度。

中国农业发展银行、中国农业银行以服务乡村振兴战略为统领，在落实农业供给侧结构性改革、支持农业农村现代化中发挥重要作用。

大型商业银行积极对接"一带一路"建设等重大区域战略、制造强国等重大国家战略；建立健全普惠金融组织机制，加大对小微、"三农"、扶贫等薄弱领域的金融支持；完善绿色金融体系，深入推进绿色发展。

中国邮政储蓄银行在实践中摸索新时期中国普惠金融新规律、新机制和新特点，充分发挥网络、资金和专业优势，构建社区金融服务生态圈，助力"三农"、小微发展，落实脱贫攻坚。

支持补短板

股份制商业银行不断加大"一带一路"金融服务力度，深化科技金融创新，支持新技术、新产品、新业态、新模式"四新"经济；大力落实普惠金融，深入分析小微企业融资的难点痛点，有效利用金融科技（Fintech）新兴技术，支持小微企业发展；加大绿色金融创新力度，助力环境友好与生态文明。

城市商业银行、农村商业银行、农村信用社联合社和村镇银行落实农业供给侧结构性改革的各项政策，深度融合地区实际及产业特色，为"三农"提供全面优质服务；积极践行双创，多策并举支持小微企业发展。

资产管理公司为中国企业在"一带一路"沿线国家开展国际产能合作、基础设施建设提供个性化、特色化、差异化的金融解决方案；支持农业现代化、集约化发展项目，助力农业安全和食品安全。

外资银行持续服务"一带一路"建设，加大"三农"、小微支持力度，推动可持续金融发展。

（二）支持区域协调发展

银行业金融机构深入贯彻落实党中央、国务院关于区域发展战略的部署，充分合理配置金融资源，深化综合金融服务，以疏解北京非首都功能为着力点，推动京津冀协同发展，落实高起点规划、高标准建设雄安新区；以绿色创新驱动发展为引领，支持长江经济带建设。继续推动中部地区崛起，支持东部地区率先发展，助力东北老工业基地振兴。

支持雄安新区发展

国家开发银行、政策性银行以及中国银行等大型商业银行主动对接国家雄安新区重大部署，加强组织领导，制定投融资规划，精准化对接新区需求，积极服务新区建设，利用多样化服务渠道大力支持雄安新区基础设施、产业融资、生态环境、特色小镇等建设，不断提高新区金融服务能力。截至 2017 年底，国家开发银行完成起步区征拆安置项目预授信 **1 774** 亿元；中国农业发展银行已审批支持雄安新区建设项目 **2** 个，审批额度 **809** 亿元，发放林业贷款项目 **1** 个，贷款余额 **1.25** 亿元；中国银行向雄安新区提供了 **220** 亿元拆迁补偿专项授信。

支持京津冀协同发展

政策性银行、中国工商银行、中国农业银行、中国银行等大型商业银行围绕京津冀协同发展国家战略，运用综合化金融服务手段，加快金融产品和服务创新，着力为京津冀轨道、高速公路、生态建设、非首都功能疏解、产业升级转移等重大项目和民生工程提供金融支持，促进京津冀优势互补、产业升级和创新发展。截至 2017 年底，中国农业发展银行支持天津、河北林业项目 **36** 个，审批贷款 **235.54** 亿元，发放贷款 **116.13** 亿元；中国农业银行对京津冀协同发展领域客户授信 **4 851** 亿元；中国银行支持京津冀协同发展项目 **418** 个，贷款余额 **2 772** 亿元。

支持长江经济带建设

政策性银行、中国银行等大型商业银行、兴业银行等股份制银行不断创新金融服务，优化信贷资源配置，积极践行绿色金融，助力沿江产业结构优化升级、长江水资源保护和合理利用，实施长江生态环境、新型城镇化建设、基础设施建设等项目，为长江经济带建设贡献力量。**兴业银行**全资子公司兴业金融租赁公司参与了金融租赁服务长江经济带战略联盟，该联盟与长江经济带域内 **11** 家省市发改委签署《战略合作协议》，将在长江绿色生态走廊、船型标准化、综合立体交通、产业转型升级、新型城镇化等方面给予长江经济带区域不低于 **3 000** 亿元的意向性租赁支持。截至 2017 年底，**中国银行**在长江沿线累计新增支援"长江经济带"项目授信 **663.8** 亿元，全年授信余额新增 **268.4** 亿元；**中国邮政储蓄银行**长江经济带地区贷款余额为 **3 100.65** 亿元。

支持中西部发展

政策性银行中国农业发展银行、中国农业银行等大型商业银行、中国邮政储蓄银行、中信银行等股份制银行、**重庆银行**等城市商业银行加大对西部地区的信贷投放力度，设立新型城镇基金，优化区域经济贷款结构，积极支持基础设施建设和特色优势产业发展，促进企业转型，全力支持中西部经济高质量增长和经济结构转型发展。截至 2017 年底，**中国农业银行**西部地区贷款余额 **24 066.26** 亿元；**中国邮政储蓄银行**西部大开发区域贷款余额 **1 896.99** 亿元；**中信银行**西部地区的贷款余额 **3 891.52** 亿元。

中国农业发展银行支持重庆沙坪坝地区西永整体城镇化"两区同建"项目

中国工商银行投贷联动支持的贵阳轨道交通 PPP 项目

招商银行支持西部地区公路建设

支持东北老工业基地振兴

国家开发银行与国家发展改革委签署《共同推进东北老工业基地振兴战略合作协议》，与 **40** 余家金融机构共同发起"东北振兴金融合作机制"。**交通银行**等大型商业银行积极支持东北地区基础设施建设、产业升级、棚户区改造等重点领域和薄弱环节。**中国邮政储蓄银行**重点支持东北老工业地区的高速公路、机场建设、风电开发、铁路建设等项目，截至 2017 年底，该行东北地区贷款余额为 **432.10** 亿元。

哈尔滨银行、辽宁省农村信用社联合社等银行业金融机构促进资源型城市建立，不断改善金融服务，创新信贷模式，加大信贷投放力度，助力东北地区供给侧结构性改革和普惠金融建设。

（三）推动对外开放发展

银行业金融机构主动适应对外开放的新形势，统筹推进服务"一带一路"顶层规划，不断提升跨境融资能力，制定多项信贷政策及措施，通过银团贷款、对外承包工程贷款、互惠贷款等多样化的金融工具，合理引导信贷投放；开展业务创新、制度创新和管理创新，为中外资企业提供多元化金融服务；积极做好应对服务"一带一路"风险防范，深化与"一带一路"国家金融同业合作，参与金融基础设施建设，为全面服务对外开放发展提供金融引擎。

国家开发银行及政策性银行在优化双边和多边合作、提供投融资支持、促进企业和产业"走出去"和"引进来"等方面发挥重要作用；中国工商银行、中国银行等大型商业银行积极完善全球服务网络，主动适应客户的多元化金融服务需求，通过跨境并购贷款、跨境资金池、境外直贷等系列产品组合支持企业"走出去"；股份制银行和城市商业银行不断加大优质信贷项目储备力度，打造境内外融资和支付结算平台，为客户提供综合的金融解决方案。截至 2017 年底，共有 10 家中资银行在 26 个"一带一路"沿线国家设立了 68 家一级机构，外资银行在华营业性机构总数 1 013 家，总资产为 3.24 万亿元人民币。[①]

推进全球布局　截至 2017 年底，中国工商银行在全球 45 个国家和地区设立 419 家机构，通过参股南非标准银行集团间接覆盖撒哈拉以南 20 个非洲国家，与 143 个国家和地区的 1 545 家境外机构建立了代理行关系；中国建设银行总行级代理行达到 1 371 家，覆盖 132 个国家和地区，基本覆盖"一带一路"沿线国家；交通银行与"一带一路"沿线 55 个国家的 515 家银行建立代理行关系；中国邮政储蓄银行共建立代理行 997 家，其中，覆盖"一带一路"沿线国家 40 个、银行 240 个；华夏银行"一带一路"沿线代理行 739 家。

深化自贸区建设　中国银行不断加大对上海自贸区建设的支持力度，截至 2017 年底，开立自由贸易账户逾 15 000 户，叙做跨境人民币借款 130 亿元，帮助上千家企业在自贸区快速发展；上海浦东发展银行积极落实上海自贸区金融支持政策，致力于支持科创中心建设、进一步拓展 FT 账户功能、扩大人民币跨境使用、建设面向国际的金融要素市场；广发银行立足服务港澳地区，助力建设粤港澳大湾区，推进前海、南沙、横琴自由贸易试验区建设；上海银行充分整合利用境内外资源、自贸区创新政策，打造跨境金融服务平台，支持上海科创中心、自由贸易港建设。

开展国际结算　截至 2017 年底，中国农业发展银行办理跨境人民币业务结算量 31.54 亿元，中国银行国际结算量为 38 300 亿元；中国建设银行国际结算量 1.17 万亿美元，境内外跨境人民币结算量 20 500 亿元；交通银行办理跨境人民币结算业务量 20 035.39 亿元；中国光大银行共办理跨境人民币结算业务 11 398 笔，合计金额 249.14 亿元；上海浦东发展银行跨境人民币结算量超过 4 500 亿元。

支持企业"走出去"　截至 2017 年底，中国进出口银行"一带一路"信贷项目共计 1 448 个，广泛分布于沿线 50 多个国家，贷款余额 7 000 多亿元人民币；中国工商银行已累计支持企业"走出去"项目 358 个，合计承贷金额 945 亿美元；中国银行累计支持中资企业"走出去"项目约 4 205 个，提供贷款承诺超过 2 805 亿美元；中国建设银行在"一带一路"沿线国家已累计储备 268 个重大项目，遍布 50 个国家和地区，投资金额 4 660 亿美元。

防范金融风险　中国进出口银行加强国别风险动态监测工作，试点对包括巴基斯坦、柬埔寨、老挝等 10 个"一带一路"国家在内的重点国家进行国别风险监测量化管理；中国工商银行积极支持"一带一路"倡议，服务中资企业在"一带一路"沿线国家的经贸、投资项目，通过跨境并购贷款、跨境资金池、境外直贷、风险参贷、内保外贷等系列产品组合支持企业"走出去"；中国农业银行设立"走出去"专项资金，完善"走出去"相关制度，完善国别风险限额管理；华夏银行在助推"一带一路"倡议过程中，加强跨境业务的信用风险、国别风险和环境、社会风险管理；广发银行针对国内服务"一带一路"地区外贸企业国际结算业务繁杂、周期过长的痛点，创新推出"跨境瞬时通"系列产品，真正实现进出口业务的全流程无纸化服务，极大提高企业国际结算效率，有效防范贸易欺诈风险。

---

① 数据来源：中国银行保险监督管理委员会。

中国工商银行支持中国船厂建造的世界最大矿砂船，将服务于巴西到中国的铁矿石运输航线

▶ 银行业在行动

国家开发银行举办欧亚经济论坛金融合作分会、第三届对非投资论坛、金砖国家银行合作机制年会、中国—东盟银联体第七次会议和基础设施互联互通金融论坛、中澳CEO圆桌会议、第十八届国际顾问委员会、上合银联体研讨会等国际会议。与中东欧 **13** 家金融机构共同发起设立中国—中东欧银联体，旨在通过建立"16+1合作"机制下的新型多边金融合作机制，更加合理、有效地整合金融资源，共同为区域内重大项目提供长期有效的投融资支持，促进中国—中东欧国家经济社会可持续发展。

中国进出口银行作为"一带一路"国际合作高峰论坛筹委会成员单位，紧密配合有关部委工作，积极参与高峰论坛的各项工作。在高峰论坛中，签订 **28** 项贷款协议，贷款总金额约 **425** 亿元，涉及交通、电力、通信、装备制造、国际产能与金融合作等多个领域，设立 **1 300** 亿元等值人民币专项贷款额度，支持"一带一路"基础设施建设、产能、金融合作。

中国工商银行举办银行家圆桌会议，形成《"一带一路"银行家圆桌会议北京联合声明》，提出以"机制共建、利益共享、责任共担、合作共赢"为基础，建立"一带一路"银行间常态化合作机制。中国银行配合国家《深化粤港澳合作推进大湾区建设框架协议》，建立支持粤港澳大湾区发展的组织机制，成立"粤港澳联动发展委员会"，促进粤港澳机构间的业务联动，推动实现区域间客户一体化服务和信息系统的互联互通，助力粤港澳大湾区建设。

招商银行举办"一带一路离岸金融服务专题研讨会"，邀请数十家开展海外项目投资及承包的中资企业，共同探讨"一带一路"建设中的金融服务需求与解决方案。2017年，该行先后与 **40** 家相关企业开展海外项目融资对接，涉及印度尼西亚、孟加拉国、越南、赞比亚等"一带一路"沿线国家。

沟通合作

交通银行响应共建"一带一路"倡议，深化与包括柬埔寨在内的东盟国家的金融合作，顺利完成人民币对柬埔寨瑞尔首发交易。图为人民币对柬埔寨瑞尔银行间市场区域交易启动仪式。

广西壮族自治区农村信用社联合社积极服务中国—东盟博览会，提供英语、粤语、客家语等多语种特色服务，架起了一座广西农信与国内外客商之间沟通的桥梁。

国家开发银行大力支持"一带一路"建设中的基础设施、能源资源、新能源等领域,重点支持了中哈(哈萨克斯坦)产能合作机制项下一系列重大重点项目、巴基斯坦胡布电站、柬埔寨暹粒机场、英国 HPC 核电、巴基斯坦贾母皮尔地区风电项目、秘鲁圣加旺三号水电站等项目。其中,秘鲁圣加旺三号水电站是中资企业在拉美高端市场特许经营、绿地项目,具有良好的示范意义。

中国工商银行作为牵头行筹组银团为巴基斯坦萨希瓦尔燃煤电站项目提供 **14.4** 亿美元贷款,该项目是中巴经济走廊投产的大型高效清洁煤电项目,年发电量预计约 **90** 亿千瓦时,可以有效缓解当地的电力短缺现状,促进巴基斯坦民生改善和经济社会发展。

重大项目落地

中国银行作为牵头行为中东地区燃煤电厂——迪拜哈翔清洁能源电站项目、西非最大的人造商用海港——加纳特马港口建设项目等一系列重大项目提供融资支持,参与中国高铁、核电、特高压、4G 通信等优势产业"走出去"。

兴业银行加大对重大港口、重大铁路、海运物流和临港产业等的金融支持力度,充分发挥该行在银行、信托、基金等领域的综合优势,对"一带一路"倡议涉及的西部 **9** 个省区市的基础设施建设,提供金融支持。

中国民生银行"新筑铁路综合物流中心项目"成功落地,
助力"一带一路"倡议建设

民生改善

截至 2017 年底,**国家开发银行**非洲中小企业专项贷款业务覆盖 **32** 个国家,累计承诺贷款 **41.9** 亿美元,发放 **19.4** 亿美元。贷款资金支持了非洲农林牧渔、加工制造、贸易流通等与民生紧密相关的行业领域,直接为当地创造就业机会 **8.7** 万个,间接使 **47** 万农户受益,带动贸易额 **20.3** 亿美元。

广西北部湾银行紧扣边境小微企业和边民特点,推动微贷业务产品创新和小微金融数据化、场景化、模型化业务体系建设,大力支持沿边科技型中小企业金融服务融资,2017 年支持沿边科技型中小企业金融服务融资余额 **7 146** 万元;为边民互市口岸量身打造的"跨境电子结算平台"正式启用,可为边境企业提供便利的线上结售汇、跨境人民币收结、反洗钱、国际收支申报与服务;出台短期出口信保项下应收账款买断业务等制度,加强与中国出口信用保险公司合作,对中信保入围免保费的出口小微企业开展授信支持,2017 年完成出口信保融资业务金额 **32** 万美元。

广西壮族自治区农村信用社联合社积极主动推进与越南商业银行同业合作,着力支持国际边贸口岸建设。截至 2017 年底,相继与越南三家商业银行签订了边贸结算业务合作协议,与越南三家商业银行合作的边贸结算业务量为 **12.37** 亿元;大力支持边贸口岸建设,2017 年共计发放口岸建设贷款 **3.51** 亿元,支持宁明、靖西、凭祥、弄怀、东兴、龙州等六家口岸建设,支持口岸农业企业开展跨国经营。

2017 年,该社累计支持"一带一路"企业 **66** 家,发放贷款 **61** 亿元,同比多支持 **25** 家,多发放 **38** 亿元。积极响应自治区政府关于"维护边境稳定,促进边境贸易和谐持续发展"的政策精神,创新开发边民贷款产品,加大对边民生产生活的信贷投入,不断提升边民金融服务工作质效。截至 2017 年底,龙州、大新等 8 家边境县级农合机构边民贷款余额 **26.96** 亿元,边民贷款户数 **35 534** 户。

中国农业银行与刚果（布）政府合作，组建中刚非洲银行并签署《刚果共和国与中国农业银行深化金融战略合作及跨境人民币金融服务协议》。中刚非洲银行致力于拓展人民币贸易结算和汇兑业务，努力实现人民币在中部非洲地区的应用及推广。

中国银行持续巩固人民币跨境流通的主渠道地位，服务企业跨境贸易和投资，引领人民币国际化产品和服务创新，促进人民币国际货币功能的发挥，推动人民币国际地位稳步提升。2017 年，新增加纳塞地、斯里兰卡卢比、孟加拉塔卡等 **13** 个新兴市场货币报价能力，非人民币外汇报价币种达到 **61** 个。在中国人民银行指定的 23 家清算行中，中国银行占 **11** 席，完成跨境人民币清算 **349.68** 万亿元、结算 **3.83** 万亿元；作为主承销商协助境外主权及类主权机构、境外非金融企业、境外金融机构等共 12 家发行人在银行间市场发行熊猫债，参与发行规模 **370** 亿元。

上海浦东发展银行积极践行人民币国际化，响应资本"引进来"号召，利用全口径宏观审慎政策支持，推出海外直贷业务 2.0 版本，服务企业从境外引入低成本资金，帮助其降低财务成本；满足人民币跨境管理需求，结合上海自贸区政策改革和创新，推出了全功能型跨境双向人民币资金池服务，为实体经济的发展和人民币国际化注入了新的活力。配合 CIPS 系统上线，提升 CIPS 系统在国际同业市场的认知度和参与度。

人民币国际化

（四）助力创新驱动发展

银行业金融机构始终坚持问题导向，聚焦制造业发展的难点痛点，着力加强对制造业科技创新、转型升级的金融支持。推进建设先进制造业融资事业部、科技金融专营机构等，提升金融服务专业化、精细化水平；创新发展符合制造业特点的信贷管理体制和金融产品体系，积极满足创新型制造业企业的资金需求。紧紧围绕"中国制造 2025"重点领域和关键任务，改进和完善制造业金融服务，促进制造业结构调整、转型升级、提质增效。

国家开发银行积极服务"中国制造 2025"，参与国家战略性新兴产业等重点行业规划编制，开创战略性新兴产业新局面；落实军民融合发展战略，促进制造业转型升级，着力支持集成电路、新能源汽车、新材料等重点领域。2017 年，发放战略性新兴产业贷款 **3 443** 亿元，同比增长 **45.2%**。

大型商业银行紧紧围绕国家科技创新的路线图和产业链布局，全力探索支持战略性新兴产业新模式，积极发展和完善助力制造强国建设的多元化金融组织体系。截至 2017 年底，中国农业银行当年新增战略性新兴产业贷款 **457** 亿元，中国银行战略性新兴产业信贷余额 **4 931** 亿元。

上海浦东发展银行设立"1+6"总行级科技金融中心，采用集约化经营方式，由总行中心牵头协调推进全行科技金融专营体制机制建设，打造"全方位、专业化、一站式"的数字化综合金融服务平台，不断升级科技金融服务方案，服务科技创新企业发展。平安银行打造规模 **250.11** 亿元的科技城产业发展基金，大力支持科技生产线项目。浙商银行与浙江省智能制造专家委员会深入合作，创新"融资、融物、融服务"的智能制造专业服务方案，运用买方信贷、设备外包、融资租赁等模式培育海洋高端装备制造业、临港先进制造业的快速发展，助推海洋产业体系优化升级。

北京银行、重庆银行等城市商业银行积极向高端制造、物联网、生物制药等领域配置信贷资源，提供并购贷款、结构性融资等一揽子金融服务，重点支持重大创新发展工程项目、科技重大专项项目、科技龙头骨干企业，切实助力创新驱动发展战略落地。

二. 创新模式 致力普惠金融

大力发展普惠金融，是我国全面建成小康社会的必然要求。银行业金融机构将践行普惠金融与自身转型发展相结合，积极探索商业可持续性，打造普惠金融产品服务体系，加强金融基础设施建设，提升科技运用水平，搭建互联网金融服务平台，提升薄弱领域金融的可得性，完善普惠金融生态环境，不断提高广大人民群众对金融服务的获得感。

（一）建设普惠金融体系

银行业金融机构不断深化普惠金融事业部建设，下沉普惠金融网点，拓展普惠金融服务网络，建立健全普惠金融服务体系机制，提升普惠金融服务能力，引导金融资源向重点领域和薄弱环节倾斜，助力实现广覆盖、多层次的机构供给体系，疏通金融活水，打通金融服务的"最后一公里"。

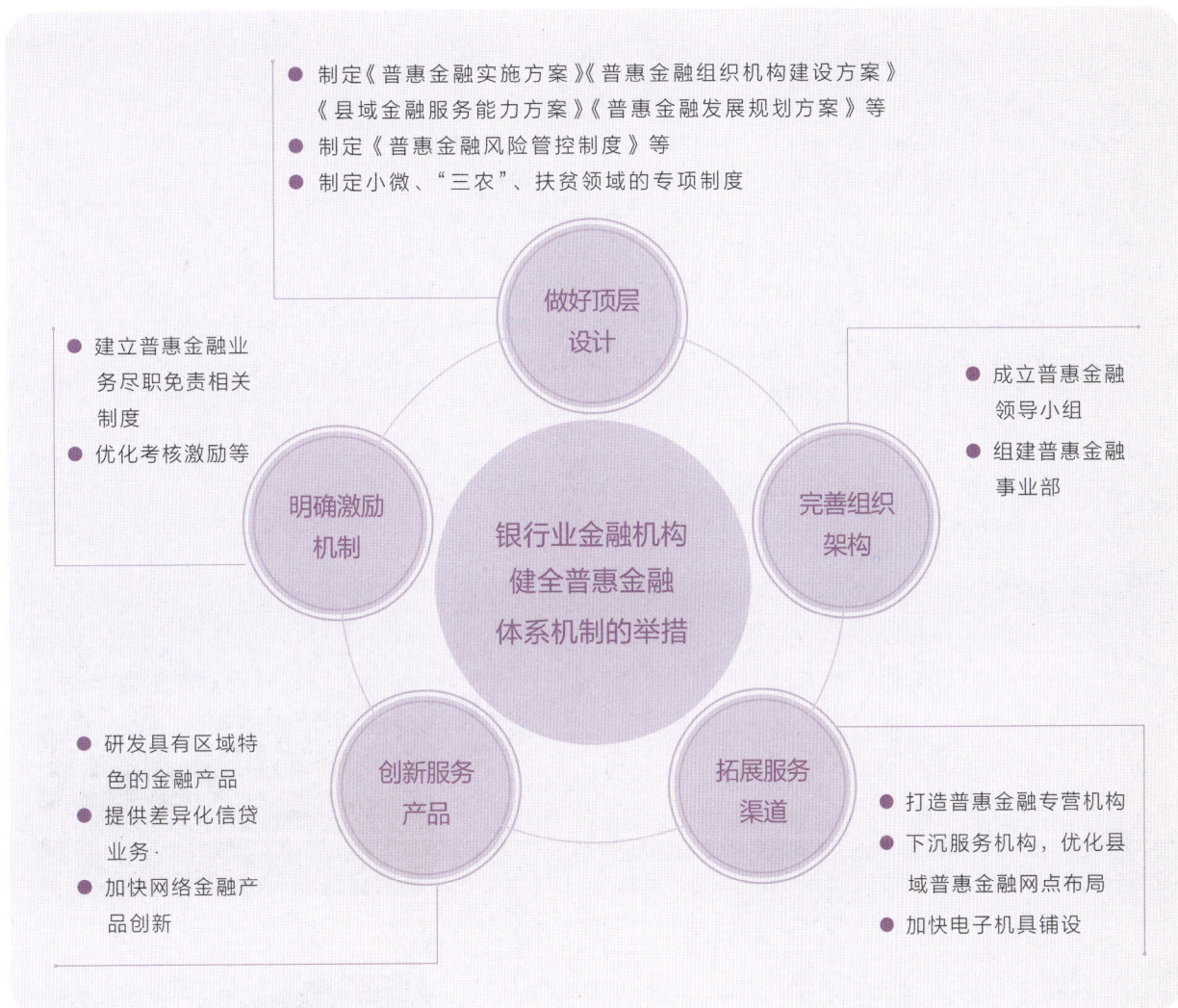

- 制定《普惠金融实施方案》《普惠金融组织机构建设方案》《县域金融服务能力方案》《普惠金融发展规划方案》等
- 制定《普惠金融风险管控制度》等
- 制定小微、"三农"、扶贫领域的专项制度

做好顶层设计

- 建立普惠金融业务尽职免责相关制度
- 优化考核激励等

明确激励机制

银行业金融机构健全普惠金融体系机制的举措

完善组织架构

- 成立普惠金融领导小组
- 组建普惠金融事业部

- 研发具有区域特色的金融产品
- 提供差异化信贷业务
- 加快网络金融产品创新

创新服务产品

拓展服务渠道

- 打造普惠金融专营机构
- 下沉服务机构，优化县域普惠金融网点布局
- 加快电子机具铺设

▶ 银行业在行动

中国农业银行在总行董事会层面设立"三农"金融／普惠金融发展委员会；在高级管理层层面设立"三农"及普惠金融事业部管理委员会；设立与普惠金融事业部与8个中后台支持中心。在首批16个"中国制造2025"试点示范城市（群）实现普惠金融服务机构全覆盖。

中国邮政储蓄银行在全国推广"三农"金融事业部改革，建立"四级架构＋三个层级"的管理机制，及"七个独立＋两个倾斜"的运行机制，业务领域实现批零联动，服务范围实现对各种农业经营主体的全覆盖，并内嵌信贷审查审批职能，提高业务办理效率。

（二）助力精准扶贫脱贫

银行业金融机构作为扶贫重要力量，充分发挥开发性、政策性、商业性和合作性金融的多元化优势和互补作用，瞄准脱贫攻坚的重点人群和重点任务，深入实施东西部扶贫协作，聚焦"三区三州"等深度贫困地区，因地制宜创新扶贫授信服务和融资模式，精准满足建档立卡贫困户易地搬迁安置、产业发展、上学就业等各类融资需求，注重提升脱贫内生发展动力，培育贫困地区"造血"功能，为实现到2020年打赢脱贫攻坚战、全面建成小康社会目标提供有力有效的金融支撑。

国家开发银行坚持"融制、融资、融智"的"三融"扶贫策略和"易地扶贫搬迁到省、基础设施到县、产业发展到村（户）、教育资助到户（人）"的"四到"思路方法，2017年开展脱贫攻坚"三大行动"，切实加大对贫困地区和人口的支持力度；政策性银行认真贯彻金融扶贫指导思想和目标要求，支持国家级贫困县摘帽和建档立卡贫困村退出，特别把贫困地区中的革命老区、定点扶贫县和政策性金融扶贫实验示范区作为重中之重，持续创新扶贫机制体制；中国银行、交通银行等大型商业银行综合运用信贷投入、资源整合、撮合引进、咨询培训等方式，不断探索商业可持续的金融扶贫有效模式；农村商业银行、农村信用社联合社等银行业金融机构精准对接省内深度贫困地区脱贫攻坚的金融服务需求，有效支持极贫乡镇基础设施建设及人居环境治理。

截至 2017 年底[1]

扶贫小额信贷余额

2 496.96 亿元

支持建档立卡贫困户

607.44 万户

贫困县行政村基础金融服务覆盖率达

95.83%

较年初提高

2.93 个百分点

▶ 银行业在行动

国家开发银行充分发挥开发性金融引领作用，以扶贫金融事业部作为决战脱贫攻坚的"集团军"，稳步推进易地扶贫搬迁。与有关部委和地方政府密切协作，贯彻落实国务院部分省份易地扶贫搬迁工作推进会、全国易地扶贫搬迁现场会议精神，有力保障全国易地搬迁资金需求；高度关注深度贫困地区脱贫攻坚，跟踪推动西藏、贵州、云南及"三区三州"等重点区域的重点项目；创新支持广西国家储备林扶贫项目，带动林区建档立卡搬迁人口脱贫。2017年，新增发放易地扶贫搬迁贷款 **560** 亿元，累计承诺 **4 483** 亿元，惠及 **911** 万建档立卡贫困人口。

国家开发银行支持武冈市易地扶贫搬迁项目

易地扶贫搬迁

中国农业发展银行严格对接国家和省级"十三五"易地扶贫搬迁规划，制定《中国农业发展银行易地扶贫搬迁专项贷款办法（2017年修订）》，进一步完善易地扶贫搬迁信贷政策，确保贷款合法合规；加大扶贫优惠政策，积极支持深度贫困地区易地扶贫搬迁；发挥地方政府组织优势、地缘优势和政策性银行融资优势，为易地扶贫搬迁后续产业发展创新信贷支持新路径。截至2017年底，易地扶贫搬迁贷款余额 **2 538.58** 亿元，惠及 **768** 万搬迁人口，其中建档立卡搬迁人口 **524** 万人。

中国农业发展银行支持四川省通江县易地扶贫搬迁项目

广西北部湾银行积极响应《田阳县"十三五"易地扶贫搬迁规划》，授信 **5 000** 万元弥补百色市移民安置小区项目建设的资金缺口，全面助力田阳县 **13 183** 户的 **45 180** 名贫困人口实施移民搬迁。

重庆农村商业银行结合扶贫小额信贷政策，制定"贫困扶助贷"专属信贷产品，着力支持贫困区县高山生态扶贫搬迁。

① 数据来源：中国银行保险监督管理委员会。

电商扶贫

中国工商银行针对贫困地区农产品销售难、好产品"养在深闺无人识"等情况，充分利用互联网金融手段，帮助优质农产品上线"融e购"网上商城销售，大力推动电商扶贫。中国建设银行打造善融商务扶贫平台，2017年善融商务实现扶贫交易额超 51 亿元，累计拥有商户 1 900 余户，覆盖 500 多个贫困县。

中国光大银行通过"云南·购精彩"平台，将电商精准扶贫模式复制到全国多个省份，成功探索出电商扶贫新路径。截至 2017 年底，"购精彩"系列电商平台精准扶贫栏目累计销售商品超 2 万件，销售额近 600 万元。

中国光大银行"云南·购精彩"电商平台助力
怒江长毛米销售

广西壮族自治区农村信用社联合社积极开展"党旗领航·电商扶贫"行动，发挥遍布全区金融服务网点以及全国农信系统点多、面广、客户众多的资源优势，为农产品提供网络销售平台，帮助贫困农户将灵山茂谷柑、荔枝、贺州三华李、百色芒果、容县沙田柚等农特产品远销 25 个省，促进农户增产增收。

光伏扶贫

中国农业银行不断丰富特色扶贫产品，立足贫困地区良好的光伏发电自然基础，积极推动光伏扶贫模式。截至 2017 年底，光伏扶贫贷款余额 25 亿元，支持项目 235 个，带动 15.6 万贫困人口增收，其中直接支持 1.7 万贫困户安装户用光伏发电系统。

中国邮政储蓄银行开发光伏扶贫小额贷款产品，陆续在山西、安徽、河北等 26 个省市试点开办光伏扶贫小额贷款，有效解决农户缺少安装发电设备资金的难题。截至 2017 年底，累计发放光伏扶贫小额贷款近 6 300 笔，金额超过 3.58 亿元。

江苏银行等城市商业银行走访省重点帮扶县（区）扶贫办、发改委以及光伏扶贫项目实施企业，深入开展调研摸底，结合现有光伏和光伏产业基金等产品，针对村级电站及政府分布式电站等不同项目类型，制定相应融资方案，加大金融精准扶贫贷款投放力度。

辽宁省农村信用社联合社贷款 2 500 万元支持建昌县光伏产业发展，有效利用当地光照时间长、太阳能资源丰富的优势，带动 1.1 万名贫困人口实现脱贫目标。

旅游扶贫

中信银行、浙商银行等股份制银行通过挖掘各地资源禀赋，积极创新推出"民宿贷"等产品，主动支持贫困地区旅游扶贫开发。

北京银行引入旅游委等专业机构，针对民俗旅游户推出民俗旅游户信用贷，助力旅游资源丰富的贫困乡村地区脱贫致富。

浙江稠州商业银行立足当地人文环境特点，以扶持民宿、工艺品等文化旅游产业探索精准扶贫。截至 2017 年底，该行累计发放 1.2 亿元贷款支持衢州根雕工艺发展，助力中国根雕文化产业园建设，推动群众脱贫致富。

浙江省农村信用社联合社、内蒙古自治区农村信用社联合社等金融机构积极开发乡村旅游资源，创新旅游扶贫信贷支持模式，加大休闲农业、乡村旅游等农村牧区一二三产业的深度融合发展，带动贫困户脱贫和就业。

（三）提升"三农"金融服务

银行业金融机构认真落实党中央乡村振兴战略，坚持以农业供给侧结构性改革为主线，以解决发展不平衡不充分问题为重点，积极推动各类涉农银行业机构回归本源，服务维护国家粮食安全、农业农村基础设施建设、农业农村现代化等领域，创新探索适合新型农业经营主体的服务方式，不断健全农村金融体系，激活农村金融市场，为书写好中华民族伟大复兴的"三农"新篇章积极贡献金融新动能。

截至 2017 年底[1]

涉农贷款余额	同比增长	其中，农户贷款余额	同比增长
30.95 万亿元	**9.64%**	**8.11** 万亿元	**14.41%**

▶ 银行业在行动

中国农业发展银行明确农业政策性银行的职责定位，出台《中国农业发展银行关于服务乡村振兴战略的指导意见》，将服务乡村振兴战略作为新时代的核心职责和中心任务，加大对乡村振兴中长期信贷投入，支持农业农村现代化和绿色发展，突出保障国家粮食安全、助推绿色兴农、改善农民生产生活条件，充分发挥政策性金融的引导、补充作用，全面助力实现到 2020 年乡村振兴取得重要进展，制度框架和政策体系基本形成的阶段性目标。截至 2017 年底，该行农业农村基础设施建设中长期贷款余额 **2.53** 万亿元，全年发放各类农业现代化贷款 **988** 亿元，支持新建高标准农田 **2 197** 万亩。

中国农业银行等大型商业银行始终坚持服务"三农"、做强县域不动摇，顺应农业农村经济的新变化、新特点、新趋势，大力实施乡村振兴战略，以服务"大三农""新三农""特色三农"为重点，不断提升"三农"金融服务水平，促进农业更强、农村更美、农民更富，开启"三农"金融事业新征程。

中国邮政储蓄银行把农业经济发展、农民创收增收摆在突出位置。2017 年该行加快完善"三农"金融事业部运作机制，在全国 **27** 家分行推广完成"三农"金融事业部改革，优化服务"三农"的管理机制；按照"一县一业、一行一品"的发展思路，创新投融资模式，服务农业产业化国家重点农业龙头企业 **378** 家，覆盖率达 **30.43%**，大力提升对农业产业链核心企业及上下游客户的金融支持。截至 2017 年底，该行涉农贷款余额达 **10 542.08** 亿元，在全行贷款余额中占比达 **30.81%**。小额贷款余额 **1 564.27** 亿元，新型农业经营主体贷款结余规模较上年末增加 **130.15** 亿元，增长 **42.97%**。

广发银行、平安银行等股份制银行把握国家农业产业化发展的新趋势，利用综合金融和金融科技优势，支持农业生产技术改进、农业面源污染防治和龙头企业的产业链客群，拉动上下游农业产业生产发展，进一步彰显绿色、生态、安全、普惠的"三农"金融本质。

哈尔滨银行不断丰富惠农信贷产品体系，全方位满足"三农"融资需求。该行在全省范围内提供农村土地承包经营权、农业设施抵押贷款服务，有效盘活农村存量资产，提高农村产权资源利用效率；创新推出农民专业合作社贷款、家庭农场贷款等，建立涵盖规模种养殖大户、家庭农场、农民专业合作社、涉农龙头企业四位一体多元化的"新型农业经营主体"产品体系；创新推出"互联网＋惠农"产品丰收 e 贷，助力新型农村金融长远发展。

青岛银行立足本土优势，着重发展新型农业、海洋渔业等特色产业，充分利用海洋渔业地理区位优势，深度考察各地海洋渔业发展模式，不断创新产品应用，支持辖区内大中型水产养殖、捕捞企业融资需求，全力推进现代农业发展。截至 2017 年底，该行海洋渔业对公贷款余额 **38 770** 万元。

---

① 数据来源：中国银行保险监督管理委员会。

天津农村商业银行持续推进金融服务站、金融便民服务点建设，实现农民足不出村就可享受小额现金存取款、转账等基础金融服务，改善农村地区金融支付环境。截至 2017 年底，全辖共设立金融服务站 1 085 家，金融服务便民点 1 423 家，基本实现千人以上村庄的金融服务覆盖。

广州农村商业银行立足南粤大地，秉持服务"三农"的经营宗旨，形成由农村金融服务站、助农取款点、移动银行等组成的多元化、广覆盖的金融服务渠道，打通服务"三农"的"最后一公里"。

厦门农村商业银行积极拓宽"三农"金融服务渠道，推进实施农户建档、精准建档、农 e 贷"三合一"工作模式。截至 2017 年底，已签约无纸化、免担保的"农 e 贷"产品合同 4 159 户，贷款金额 1.57 亿元。

江西省农村信用社联合社探索开创"农商银行＋龙头企业＋农户""农商银行＋农民专业合作社＋种养大户"等信贷模式，将核心企业与优质农户结合，2017 年对接龙头企业 1 001 户、农民专业合作社 9 983 户、家庭农场 5 493 户、专业大户 22 410 户、其他新型经营主体 529 户，合计授信 207.76 亿元，带动 162 532 余户农户创业就业。

内蒙古自治区农村信用社联合社坚持立足"三农三牧"、服务城乡社区的市场定位，优先保证传统农牧业生产资金需求，重点支持粮食生产、现代畜牧业发展、农牧业产业化经营、农牧业生产经营方式创新，大力推动家庭农牧场、种养大户、专业合作社等新型农牧业经营主体发展。截至 2017 年底，全区农村信用社涉农涉牧贷款余额 1 843.77 亿元。

四川省农村信用社联合社积极推行"一次核定、随用随贷、余额控制、周转使用、动态调整"的农户信贷管理和整村推进模式，为全省 1 331 万户建立经济档案。2017 年该行向 146 万农户发放贷款 2 708 亿元，有力支持绿色种植业和养殖业发展。

甘肃省农村信用社联合社制定《关于做好 2017 年涉农贷款营销工作的指导意见》《关于做好春耕备耕金融服务工作的通知》，积极调整信贷结构，将金融资源向粮食生产、特色产业倾斜，精细对接优质、高效、绿色农业等新业态新主体需求，推动农业现代化和农村城镇化。

汇丰村镇银行高度关注并参与中国农村金融改革，始终以推动当地"三农"经济发展为己任，致力于将国际化金融服务逐步延伸至农村市场最前沿。截至 2017 年底，涉及农户及小微企业的贷款合计 11.07 亿元，占各项贷款余额的 92%。

中国邮政储蓄银行真情服务农户

国家开发银行支持中科生物现代农业植物工厂产业化项目

广西壮族自治区农村信用社联合社推出新农贷，解决种植养殖专业户在生产经营过程中的资金需求

（四）扶持小微企业成长

银行业金融机构坚持"因企施策、差异化服务"的原则，有效利用互联网、大数据、云计算、人工智能等金融科技新兴技术，不断创新个性化服务及小微信贷产品，搭建合作平台，融资融智，推进专营机构建设，提高服务质效，扩大服务覆盖面，着力破解小微企业融资难、融资贵的问题，有效促进小微企业健康发展。

截至 2017 年底[1]

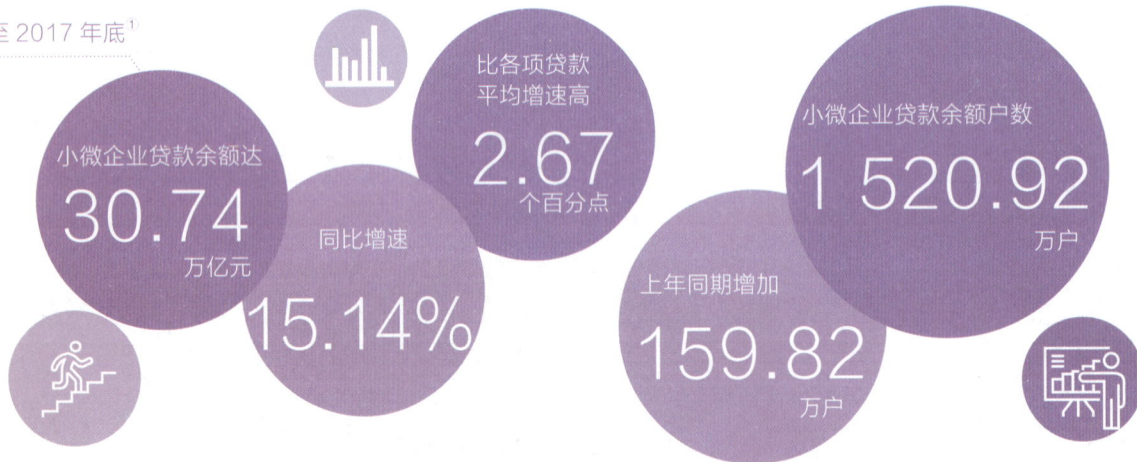

小微企业贷款余额达 **30.74** 万亿元

同比增速 **15.14%**

比各项贷款平均增速高 **2.67** 个百分点

小微企业贷款余额户数 **1 520.92** 万户

上年同期增加 **159.82** 万户

中国农业发展银行在浙江、江西积极开展"支农转贷款"业务试点工作；中国工商银行、中国银行等大型商业银行推进普惠金融网点建设，提升基层支行信贷服务能力，不断完善服务中小企业的产品服务体系；中信银行、中国光大银行、浙商银行等股份制银行倾斜授信资源，建设小微"信贷工厂"，创新续贷产品；北京银行等城市商业银行搭建小微批量合作平台，广泛开展银企、银税合作，加强专营机构建设，以产品为抓手，强化小微服务。

银行业金融机构根据市场和小微企业的融资需求，不断创新小微企业金融服务产品，在实践中探索推陈出新，形成了丰富多彩的产品服务体系，出现了中国工商银行的"工银财富贷"、中国银行的"中银接力通宝"、中国光大银行的"小微企业在线融资系统"、华夏银行的"电商贷"小微金融 APP、兴业银行"三剑客"产品组合、中国民生银行的"中小企业民生工程"、浙商银行的"点易贷"、重庆银行的"好企贷"等产品，多彩的产品体系构建起良好的生态金融体系，以灵活、快捷、高效的服务特色，提升小微企业金融服务效率。

① 数据来源：中国银行保险监督管理委员会。

中国邮政储蓄银行搭建多方共赢的合作平台，与中华人民共和国工业和信息化部、上海证券交易所、某信息股份有限公司成功签订战略合作协议，大力推进与科技、工商等部门各类合作项目，充分发挥"银政、银协、银企、银担"平台信息互动、风险共担、优势互补的优势作用，着力改善中小企业融资环境。2017年，累计发放小微企业贷款 **7 607.52** 亿元。

浙商银行建立了专门的小微金融产品研发团队，围绕小微企业主重点关心的担保方式、效率、额度、期限等问题，形成了门类齐全、种类丰富的特色产品体系。该行研发推出新兴市场的"三板贷"、投贷联动的"创赢贷"产品；创新推出"文创贷""科创贷"、开发额度灵活使用的"信用通"、针对民宿经济的"民宿贷"；推出"账户通""小微结算卡"等结算产品，大力推广"三年贷""随易贷""到期转""连续贷"等还款方式创新产品，有效解决小微企业贷款无缝周转问题。

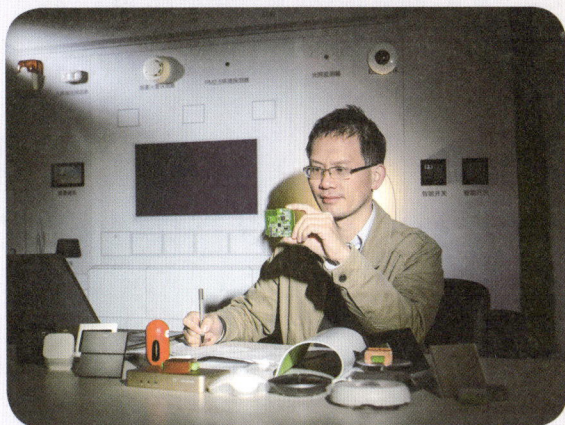

工程师杨先生在浙商银行小企业按揭数据贷的支持下
中年转型，创业智能家居

江苏银行综合考虑资金、风险、运营等成本要素，研发小微企业定价模型和系统，实行精细化定价，有效控制企业融资成本；同时，主动精简收费项目，能免则免、能减则减，并实现系统自动控制，2017年主动减免费用近 **3 000** 万元。

江西银行落实银监会《关于完善和创新小微企业贷款服务提高小微企业金融服务水平的通知》要求，出台优惠政策，创新企业客户流动资金贷款服务模式，对通过审核的企业，予以直接续贷，不再需企业通过"过桥"资金倒贷，有效降低企业融资成本，缩短了再融资审批时间。截至2017年底，该行为小微企业办理续贷余额 **132.52** 亿元，办理笔数超过 **1 634** 笔。

杭州银行创建新型申贷渠道，针对"微贷卡"业务推出了微信、手机银行APP、官网等多重电子申请渠道，针对"微贷卡""云抵贷"业务推出了二维码申请功能。客户可以通过前述电子渠道或客户经理的分享链接发起申请，还可以生成专属二维码保存，全方位提升金融服务。

恒生银行（中国）作为港资背景银行，珠三角地区一直是该行的业务发展重点。早在2009年，该行就与某出口信用保险公司开展合作，联同香港母行以及澳门分行，共同签署了横跨三地的出口信用保险银行保单。借助该银行保单，中小出口企业可以直接通过银行投保、申报和索赔，大大降低企业的管理成本；同时，企业还可以享受银行保单的优惠定价，降低企业的保费负担，这在一定程度上解决了中小企业融资中成本、收益不对称的难题。

中国建设银行走访小企业客户，了解客户生产经营情况，
为客户制定综合金融服务方案

华夏银行实地走访小企业客户

三. 把握需求
优化客户服务

（一）引领服务提质增效

（二）丰富服务渠道

（三）维护消费者权益

银行业金融机构秉承"以客为尊"的服务理念，布局服务文化战略规划，积极发挥金融科技引领作用，充分运用互联网技术和大数据分析，为客户提供更全方位的便捷服务。进一步调整优化传统网点，整合升级现有产品服务，适时推动业务转型。进一步完善消费者权益保护制度建设，将消费者权益保护融入企业经营的各个方面，构建更加有效的消费者保护工作机制，不断提升服务质效、改善客户体验。

（一）引领服务提质增效

2017年，银行业金融机构充分发挥服务文化的引领作用，多措并举，理念先行，凝练出独具匠心的特色文化，形成固化服务理念、提升服务质效、改善客户体验、展示服务形象的内生动力。

▶ 银行业在行动

助力行业服务提质增效

数字化、网络化、智能化、移动化使现代社会和经济活动变得更加灵活、便捷、智慧。金融科技成为驱动金融服务创新发展的动力，为银行业带来了新的挑战和机遇。2017年，中国银行业以科技创新为驱动力，顺应时代潮流，以"普惠、跨界、安全、效率"为主题，持续加强先进科技手段和管理方式在金融领域的推广应用，改变传统银行服务模式，助力服务效率提升，增强服务供给侧技术动能，促进银行业可持续均衡发展。

推动行业服务转型升级

面对"强监管"的新环境和不断变化的社会需求，中国银行业协会及时对文明规范服务工作进行总结，对服务标准体系进行了升级调整，保持评价体系的先进性、科学性和引领性。各银行业金融机构按照新标准完善了更新服务管理制度、优化服务组织框架，使行业整体服务质量水平得到全面提升。

培育行业服务标杆

为继续推进行业文明规范服务品牌体系建设，持续深化优质服务网点引领示范作用，不断提升行业整体服务水平和质量，中国银行业协会组织开展了2017年度中国银行业文明规范服务"百佳单位"及"星级营业网点"达标评估工作，全面展示行业服务形象。达标评估工作经过营业网点自荐申报、银行系统督导提升、地方协会考核审核、监管部门合规意见、中银协现场巡检以及业内专家会商、业内外志愿者体验测评、最终评审等多个环节，涌现出大批优秀的营业网点。荣获"百佳单位"的网点，以现代化、智能化的服务设施、高水平的服务质量，树立起行业服务标杆形象，展示了行业服务风采。

持续提升客户满意度

中国银行业通过不断创新产品服务、丰富服务渠道、完善服务流程、注重细节管理，关注消费者需求，行业整体服务能力持续提高，客户满意度稳步提升。2017年，中国消费者协会联合中国残疾人联合会在全国31个省、自治区和直辖市范围内选取 102 个城市开展了无障碍设施调查体验活动。从调查数据来看，金融服务无障碍设施满意度均达到了 75 分以上。

（二）丰富服务渠道

2017年，银行业金融机构加快自助银行的布局建设，有效延伸了传统营业网点服务半径，提升了县域金融服务能力。同时，不断致力于简流程、扩功能、提智能，为客户提供优质服务。

据不完全统计，截至 2017 年底[1]

银行业金融机构在全国布局建设自助银行	较上年增加	增幅	布放自助设备	其中创新自助设备
16.84 万家	**7 300** 多家	**4.59%**	**80.26** 万台	**11.39** 万台

---

① 数据来源：《2017年中国银行业服务报告》。

银行业金融机构自助设备交易笔数	交易总额	同比增长
400.06 亿笔	**66.13** 万亿元	**10.37%**

▶ 银行业在行动

传统网点持续优化	2017 年，中国银行业始终坚持"以客户为中心"的原则，密切关注经济金融资源和客户金融需求变化，综合分析各营业网点发展潜力，制定周密的规划，调整优化网点布局，改善设施，细化分区，提高网点单产。截至 2017 年底，全国银行业金融机构营业网点总数达到 **22.87** 万个，其中，据不完全统计，新增营业网点 **800** 多个，年内改造营业网点 **1.07** 万个。
电子渠道深化创新	2017 年，中国银行业主动顺应人工智能、大数据和区块链等移动化的发展趋势，积极运用金融科技最新成果，加快推进各类渠道的智能化转型，全面打通客户接触渠道，降低金融服务门槛，提升客户交易体验，构筑零售金融体系化竞争优势。据不完全统计，2017 年银行业金融机构离柜交易达 **2 600.44** 亿笔，同比增长 **46.33%**；离柜交易金额达 **2 010.67** 亿元，同比增长 **32.06%**；行业平均离柜业务率为 **87.58%**。
社区银行效能提升	2017 年，中国银行业坚持规范化、差异化发展战略，整合优势资源，进一步规范社区银行、小微银行的设立，网点综合营销服务能力得到增强，发展效能持续提升。据不完全统计，截至 2017 年底，中国银行业设立社区网点 **7 890** 个，小微网点达到 **2 550** 个。
加强无障碍服务	中国银行业协会根据《深化标准化工作改革方案》（国发 [2015]13 号）和"一行三会"及中国国家标准化管理委员会联合发布的《金融业标准化体系建设发展规划（2016—2020 年）》，为进一步全面提升银行业无障碍服务水平，推动我国银行业无障碍环境建设工作向制度化、规范化、标准化的纵深发展，在中国残疾人联合会等组织的协助下，2017 年，中国银行业协会组织启动了《中国银行业无障碍环境建设标准》制定工作，以规范和指引全行业金融机构更好地满足残疾人客户日益增长的金融服务需求，努力让残疾人客户共享我国金融经济社会发展成果和优质的金融服务。
智能银行引领发展	2017 年，中国银行业以智能创新推动智慧银行建设，通过各类智能技术和设备的广泛运用，逐步实现对银行传统经营模式、管理体制机制、业务体系及品牌文化的系统性智慧创新再造与重塑，在满足客户多元化服务需求的同时，引领未来转型发展。

[1] 数据来源：《2017 年中国银行业服务报告》。

客服开启智能时代

2017 年，中国银行业不断提升客户服务中心的服务水平，强化标准规范化建设，引领人工智能发展潮流，打造智能客户服务体验。据不完全统计，截至 2017 年底，银行业金融机构客服从业人员为 **5.12** 万人，全年人工处理来电 **10.73** 亿人次，服务客户数量达 **42.09** 亿人次；银行业客服中心人工电话平均接通率达 **91.22%**，其中信用卡客服专线人工接通率为 **93.37**%，连续五年高于 **90%**。

（三）维护消费者权益

2017 年，银行业金融机构认真贯彻落实《中华人民共和国消费者权益保护法》、国务院《关于加强金融消费者权益保护工作的指导意见》《中国人民银行金融消费者权益保护实施办法》和中国银监会《银行业金融机构销售专区录音录像管理暂行规定》《关于加强银行业消费者权益保护　解决当前群众关切问题的指导意见》《关于印发 2017 年银行业消费者权益保护工作要点的通知》，扎实推进本单位消费者权益保护制度体系建设，努力提高银行业消费者权益保护工作的有效性。各银行业机构通过完善流程、规范宣传、硬件保障等多措并举，认真落实销售专区、产品销售"双录"等有关要求，规范产品销售行为，完善信息公示，切实将消费者权益保护融入银行业经营管理的各个环节。

2017 年，银行业持续开展公众教育活动，各银行业金融机构在坚持公益性、时效性、服务性和持续性的原则下，主动、规范、持续、系统地开展公众教育工作。通过对社会公众进行金融知识普及、金融意识和金融素质培养，防范和化解潜在矛盾，构建和谐的金融消费环境，促进银行业健康可持续发展。

中国银行业协会连续七年组织全行业开展"普及金融知识万里行活动"。活动由"支付结算账户使用安全宣传月""电子智能服务推广宣传月""防范电信网络诈骗宣传月"三项主题活动组成。

据不完全统计，2017 年[1]

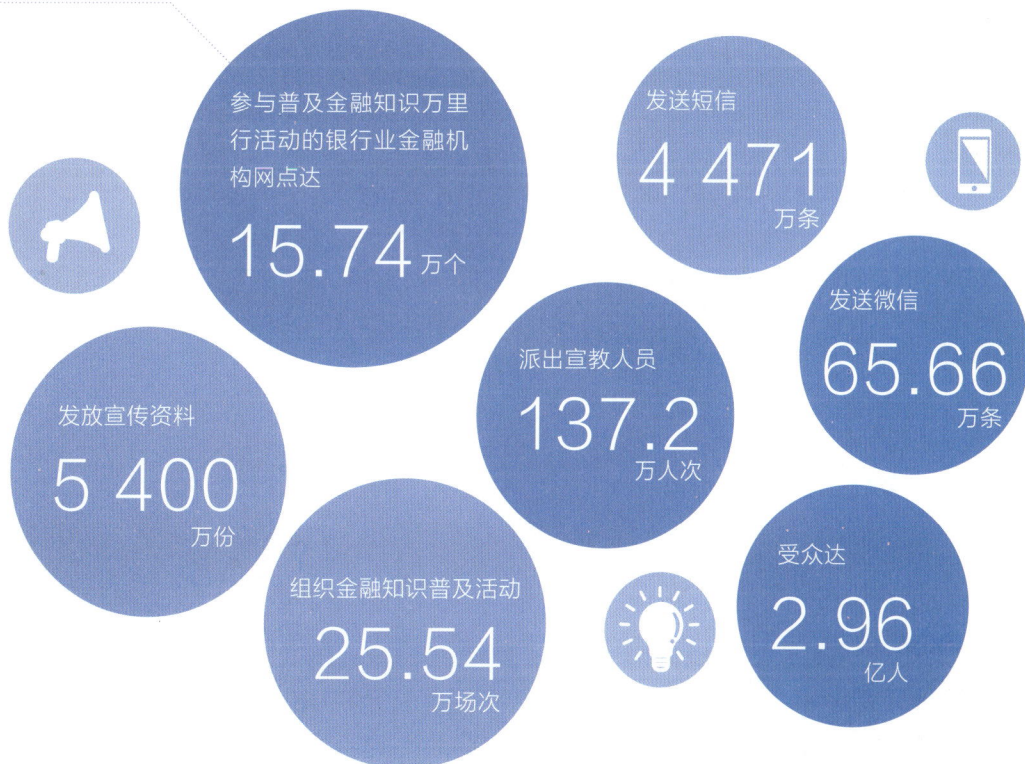

参与普及金融知识万里行活动的银行业金融机构网点达 **15.74** 万个

发送短信 **4 471** 万条

发放宣传资料 **5 400** 万份

派出宣教人员 **137.2** 万人次

发送微信 **65.66** 万条

组织金融知识普及活动 **25.54** 万场次

受众达 **2.96** 亿人

① 数据来源：《2017 年中国银行业服务报告》。

四. 保护生态 推进绿色发展

（一）发展绿色金融

（二）践行绿色低碳

银行业金融机构树立绿水青山就是金山银山的理念，支持环境改善、应对气候变化和资源节约高效利用的经济活动，加大绿色信贷投入，开展绿色办公运营，强化供应链管理，践行绿色公益环保，致力推动绿色、低碳经济发展和美丽中国建设。

中国农业发展银行支持张家口国家储备林项目

（一）发展绿色金融

银行业金融机构持续贯彻落实《关于构建绿色金融体系的指导意见》，将绿色信贷理念融入机构战略政策、组织架构、管理制度和业务流程；切实加强环境社会风险管理，完善相关信息披露；主动创新绿色金融产品服务，通过发行绿色金融债、开展绿色信贷资产转让等方式多渠道筹集资金，重点支持低碳、循环、生态领域的融资需求。

截至 2017 年 6 月末[1]

21 家主要银行

绿色信贷余额

8.22 万亿元

其中

节能环保、新能源、新能源汽车等战略新兴产业贷款余额为

1.69 万亿元

节能、环保项目和服务贷款余额为

6.53 万亿元

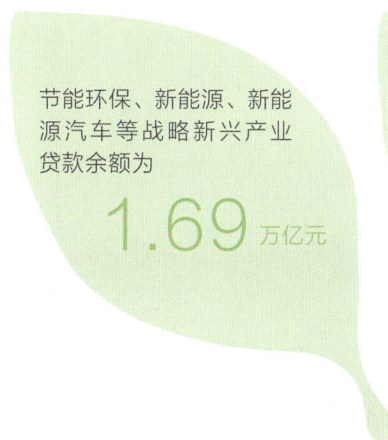

① 数据来源：中国银行保险监督管理委员会。

国家开发银行完善制度建设，规范绿色信贷、绿色金融债券发行等领域的项目尽调、授信审查、贷后管理等各环节；推进机制建设，积极参与有关部委和地方政府绿色金融相关政策和融资规划的研究制定，2017年为湖北省编制《长江经济带生态保护投融资规划》，创新模式以特许经营、PPP、政府购买服务、合同能源管理等方式支持大气污染防治、流域水环境治理等项目。截至2017年底，该行绿色信贷贷款余额 **16 423** 亿元。

中国进出口银行合理配置信贷资源，促进绿色、循环和低碳经济发展；助力钢铁等一批高能耗、高排放企业技改项目的推进；继续加大对绿色农业开发、资源循环利用、垃圾处理及污染防治、可再生能源及清洁能源、绿色交通运输、节能环保服务、工业节能节水环保等领域的支持力度。截至2017年底，该行绿色信贷余额突破 **1 000** 亿元，支持的项目合计减少标准煤使用量 **1 702.03** 万吨，二氧化碳减排量 **3 300.1** 万吨，二氧化硫减排量 **11.12** 万吨，氮氧化物减排量 **3.37** 万吨，节水 **3 202.38** 万吨，产生了显著的环保和社会效应。

完善体系

兴业银行深化与环保非政府组织"福建绿家园环境友好中心"开展合作，将其整理的《福建省污染企业名单》等环境预警信息纳入风险预警管理系统，不断推进企业环境风险预警分类机制建设，并在此基础上帮助企业排查环境风险点，提出环境整改意见，增强企业环境风险防范意识与管理能力，切实履行银行的环境和社会责任。

渤海银行制定《渤海银行授信业务环境和社会风险管理办法》，在信用风险管理系统中建立"工业转型升级、产业结构调整类型、是否国家限制行业、三高一汰、两高一资"等标识，建立健全绿色金融环境与社会风险管理体系。

汇丰银行（中国）基于赤道原则框架，在信贷申请管理中建立可持续风险评级系统，对绿色项目的影响规模和客户管理能力进行评估，简化符合要求的项目环境审批流程，提升服务效能；2017年加入陆家嘴金融城绿色责任投资原则倡议，参与绿色金融多项研讨活动，积极推动中国可持续金融发展。

广西北部湾银行支持建设玉林大容山景区风力发电厂水环境治理

林业

中国农业发展银行以张家口市全面开展植树造林、构建北京生态屏障、承办绿色奥运为契机，利用政策优势与省林业厅及当地政府对接，量身定制融资方案，支持国家储备林基地建设重点项目，促成政府设立"储备林项目建设风险偿债基金"。截至2017年底，该行发放储备林项目贷款**33.3**亿元，助力2022年冬奥会绿色奥运的生态环境建设。

交通银行成立林业调研小组，通过收集资料、定期监控、走访林业主管部门等方式制定项目授信政策，大力支持广西国有东门林场**12**万亩桉树基地造林项目，助力亚洲最大的桉树基因库建设。截至2017年底，项目固定资产贷款余额**9 800**万元。

华夏银行将森林资源培育、林下种植、林下养殖等林业项目纳入绿色信贷支持范围，助力林业资源有效开发与利用，助力地方经济增长和生态环保。

杭州银行、桂林银行等城市商业银行根据国家林业局《关于林权抵押贷款的实施意见》，通过各种创新融资担保方式盘活林业企业资产，解决其"融资难"的问题，积极支持林业发展。

清洁能源

招商银行发放贷款**4 800**万元支持黑龙江七台河市生物质能热电厂项目。该项目利用玉米秸秆资源加工生物质燃料进行发电和供热，每年可实现发电量超过**2**亿度、供热面积近**200**万平方米，年平均节约标准煤约**8**万吨，显著改善当地空气质量，为守护碧水蓝天提供金融支撑。

河北银行等城市商业银行配合国家节能减排战略，聚焦清洁能源、可再生资源的开发与利用，支持风电、光伏发电、垃圾发电等重大项目，不断加大节能环保领域的信贷投放，推动经济绿色发展。

徽商银行使用绿色债券募集资金，大力支持淮北市中湖矿山地质环境治理和马鞍山市中心城区水环境综合治理项目。其中，淮北市中湖项目包含对区域内**3.61**万亩地块的综合治理，治理完成后将形成可利用土地**2.45**万亩，水域**1.16**万亩，蓄水总容量**6 927**万立方米，有效改善当地生态环境。

江西银行所募集的绿色金融债券资金，根据资金使用规定，在2017年为芦溪县政府发放**3.5**亿元贷款，助力改善河流水环境生态系统，保障芦溪县水系中的灌溉和城镇供水安全，有效带动农家乐、观光果园等产业的发展。

建筑节能

中国建设银行武汉生产园区安装雨水综合利用系统，为园区绿化灌溉及冲洗提供用水，每年节约用水约**4 000**立方米；通过余热回收技术，采用水源热泵回收数据机房的余热，为园区提供生活热水及供暖，相比普通热水锅炉7×24小时供暖，每天可节约天然气约**5 000**立方米。

上海浦东发展银行积极参与"世界银行——长宁区建筑节能和低碳城区建设项目"，对长宁区内**150**幢**2**万平方米以上的楼宇进行节能改造，为区域内新建建筑及现有建筑的节能改造提供资金支持。截至2017年底，世界银行建筑节能转贷款项目获得**2 000**万美元竞争性额度，累计完成**6 000**万美元提款，项目已圆满完成。

产品服务创新

中国农业发展银行发行**30**亿元"债券通"绿色债券，有利于推动中国债券市场基础设施互联互通、促进上海国际金融中心及上海自由贸易港的建设。

中国工商银行于2017年9月28日创新推出"一带一路"绿色债券，积极宣传中国绿色发展理念，服务绿色"一带一路"建设；最终发行量等值**21.5**亿美元，获得国际气候与环境研究中心最高"深绿"评级以及气候债券倡议组织的"气候债券"认证。

中国建设银行持续深化与国内7家碳排放权交易所的合作，创新推出碳金融信贷产品，制定《公司业务与同业业务条线推进碳金融业务联动方案》，充分发挥"碳金融"和"碳配额远期交易中央对手清算代理业务"的产品优势，完善绿色金融产品体系建设。

上海浦东发展银行与亚洲开发银行就绿色银团贷款项目展开合作，贷款资金用于绿色动力环保集团推广在中小城市的 PPP 垃圾发电项目。

产品服务创新

北京银行2017年发行 300 亿元绿色金融债券支持节能、污染防治、资源节约与循环利用、清洁交通、清洁能源、生态保护和适应气候变化六大领域，降低绿色信贷融资成本，增强绿色产业支持力度。截至2017年底，投放的 70 余个项目贷款余额约为 160 亿元。

温州银行加强与环保部门合作，研究有关节能环保领域的经济发展特点，创新推出"小水电整体资产抵押""应收账款质押""排污权质押"等授信产品，助力绿色产业的可持续发展。

（二）践行绿色低碳

银行业金融机构积极响应国家节能减排号召，坚持"绿色发展""低碳金融"的经营理念，持续关注运营过程中产生的资源消耗和环境影响。在内部办公过程中，深入推进线上办公系统进一步降低纸张消耗；大力发展网络金融，通过在小微、个人消费信贷、信用卡等业务领域不断提高线上便捷化金融服务比例，大大降低传统线下业务办理环节的纸张消耗以及客户出行成本。

在楼宇节能减排方面，持续开展节电、节水、节油行动，提高办公用品使用和回收处理效率，如对电子废物进行安全、环保回收处理；在集中采购环节，将环境评价纳入供应商准入标准，采用达标技术、设备和材料，打造绿色办公环境；组织植树、骑行等多项绿色公益活动，构建银行绿色文化，提升员工环保意识。

中国建设银行将绿色理念纳入采购管理制度，在采购投标环节设定产品与服务的绿色准入要求和评价标准，确保供应商在生产过程中的污染物控制工作达到相关要求，致力于营造行业间绿色经营的生态环境。2017年该行召开供应商沟通交流会，邀请 23 家重点供应商代表出席，就采购项目合作中有效履行环境和社会责任深入交流和讨论。

中国民生银行强化集中采购价格、质量、供货和服务管理，优先购买可回收、可重复利用的材料和对环境负面影响小的环保标志产品；在营业办公用房建设和装修过程中，秉承"厉行节约、勤俭办行"宗旨，注重探索能耗与效率、生态与科技、集成与优化、现在与未来之间的利益共享，提高建筑使用效能，积极建设绿色银行。

中国光大银行在贵安新区金牛湖公园开展"携手创绿·共植未来"植树活动

　　上海银行从严把好供应商选择的绿色采购关,将供应商对环保材料的使用比率、产品环保技术的达标以及是否会通过改进技术、实行 ISO14001 清洁生产方式和环境管理生产模式 **4** 个方面作为优先选用和准入的重要因素,保障绿色、低碳、健康的办公环境。

广发银行南海广发金融中心绿色银行建设

金华银行组织青年员工投身"五水共治"巡河活动,清理河道垃圾

中国信达资产管理公司湖南分公司组织绿色骑行活动,传播环保理念,吸引更多利益相关方的参与,共同促进生态环境保护

三井住友银行(中国)举办"低碳出行·共建绿色家园"五里河公园健步走活动

五．以人为本 关注员工发展

（一）保护员工权益

（二）促进员工职业发展

（三）关怀员工生活

　　和谐的劳动关系有利于促进企业的良性发展。银行业金融机构坚持以人为本的理念，强化员工权益保障，为员工提供事业发展平台，开展全方位、多层次的职业能力培训，举办多彩的文体活动，加强困难员工关爱，将员工的工作生活和未来职业成长相结合，努力为员工创造乐观、积极、和谐的工作氛围。

据不完全统计，截至 2017 年底[1]

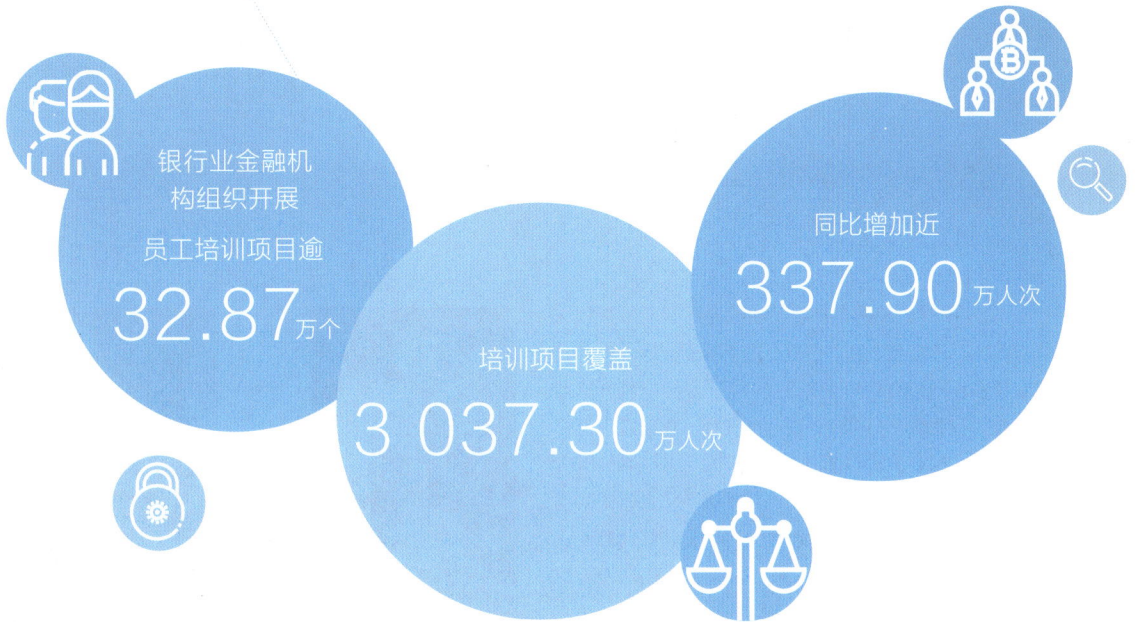

银行业金融机构组织开展

员工培训项目逾

32.87万个

培训项目覆盖

3 037.30万人次

同比增加近

337.90万人次

（一）保护员工权益

保障员工权益是企业健康发展的基础。银行业金融机构严格遵守并执行《劳动法》《劳动合同法》等相关法律法规，致力于向员工提供稳定的就业岗位、合理的薪酬福利，禁止雇佣童工，公平、公正对待不同国籍、种族、性别、宗教信仰和文化背景的员工；畅通沟通渠道，切实保障员工休息、休假、体检等各项基本权益，致力于打造尊重、多元、和谐的工作氛围，提升员工幸福感。

▶ 银行业在行动

江苏银行畅通员工"说真话、讲实话"的渠道，建好用好员工意见建议平台。2017 年，员工意见建议平台共收集意见建议 **3 606** 条，办结 **3 566** 条，占比 **98.9%**。

北京农商银行在以往固定招聘渠道基础上，开展了藏籍大学生、退役大学生士兵和军队转业干部招聘，共招录 **21** 人。

中国工商银行美国区域机构平等对待员工

桂林银行召开四届四次职工代表大会

① 数据来源：中国银行业协会。

（二）促进员工职业发展

员工职业发展是企业可持续发展的重要前提。银行业金融机构持续强化员工理论知识武装，重视员工培训和人才培养，根据业务发展需要和不同层级员工岗位需求和特点，开发设计培训项目和课程，开展员工分层、分类培训，综合运用研讨交流、案例教学、视频培训、网络培训等方式，构建覆盖面广、层次分明、针对性强的培训模式，打造多渠道、系统化的全方位培训体系，构建"人尽其用"的用人环境。

▶ 银行业在行动

上海浦东发展银行不断促进培训成果向绩效成果有效转化，聚焦跨界学习和业务创新，探索开展创新发展课程体系建设，完成整体规划框架及附属成果研发，为造就一支精通跨专业知识、熟悉跨行业常识、掌握处理复杂业务、善于跨界创新的人才队伍提供依据。该行积极引入案例开发专业技术，围绕总结实践经验、推广最佳实践、提升组织绩效，结合培训课程体系建设和重点培训项目实施，初步建立基于全行经营管理情景的案例开发和应用管理体系，为打造浦发银行内部知识共享平台、加速人才学习与成长打下扎实基础。

浙商银行搭建学习、考试、培训管理三位一体且功能完善、手机电脑灵活使用、随时随地自由学习的浙银大学智慧云平台。截至 2017 年底，该行共计组织 112 门网上课程学习，26 场考试，6 872 人参与使用，使用平台累计时长 28 555 个小时。

浙商银行"支行行长扬帆计划"培训现场，学员和导师积极互动

江苏银行组织员工开展户外拓展训练

（三）关怀员工生活

银行业金融机构持续关爱员工身心健康，平衡员工的工作和生活，建立健全员工关爱体系，加强女性员工及离退休员工关爱，开展员工心理健康讲座，完善内部员工互助会机制及医疗救助体系，加强困难员工慰问，通过开展丰富多彩的文体活动，提升员工职业幸福感。

据不完全统计，2017 年[1]

银行业金融机构共提供员工受灾补助、医疗救助、生活帮扶等各项帮扶资金逾

5.17
亿元

▶ 银行业在行动

国家开发银行 2017 年通过驻外人员心理检测、电话咨询和面对面心理咨询相结合等多种形式保障驻外员工的心理健康。

渤海银行 在总行大楼开设退休干部活动中心，作为退休干部座谈学习、了解行情、健身活动的固定场所，满足老同志活到老、学到老的愿望，共享银行发展成果。

徽商银行 为切实贯彻《安徽省女职工劳动保护条例》，进一步推动维护女职工基本权益，关爱关心女职工的工作，该行从女员工最关心、最基础的权益出发，积极参与考勤办法的讨论，召开女员工座谈会，建立总行机关母婴室、组建女员工瑜伽训练兴趣小组、协助女员工处理家庭纠纷，维护该行员工权益。

青岛银行 为进一步提升研究成果对业务发展的支撑力度，倾力打造了"研究成果分享平台"和"一线服务平台"——"乐研"论坛，主题涵盖"绿色金融视角下商业银行可持续发展研究""中国银行的明天在哪里——双轨战略""后利率市场化下的流动性风险"等。

汇丰银行（中国） 在北京、上海、广州、深圳、成都共举办十场讲座，涵盖人际沟通、亲子教育、运动养生等不同主题内容，还提供专家热线咨询。此外，该行多元共融小组组织员工习练易筋经、习练养生健身气功，使员工在工作之余，品味不同生活。

中国农业发展银行开展员工心理讲座

招商银行举办"奔跑吧招行"123 一起跑·全国接力挑战赛

富滇银行在"三八·妇女节"期间开展"快乐彩跑庆三八"活动

① 数据来源：中国银行业协会。

六．赤诚之心
投身公益事业

银行业金融机构秉承"责任银行、和谐发展"的社会责任理念，追求经济利益与社会利益的快速协同发展，践行社会主义核心价值观，深入推进各项公益慈善事业发展。2017年，银行业金融机构持续完善公益管理体系，积极推进社会公益项目建设，促进客户以多元化方式参与公益项目。通过建立系统化公益管理体系和长效性公益项目，切实履行社会责任，为建设幸福中国，实现"中国梦"贡献卓越力量。

据不完全统计，2017 年[1]

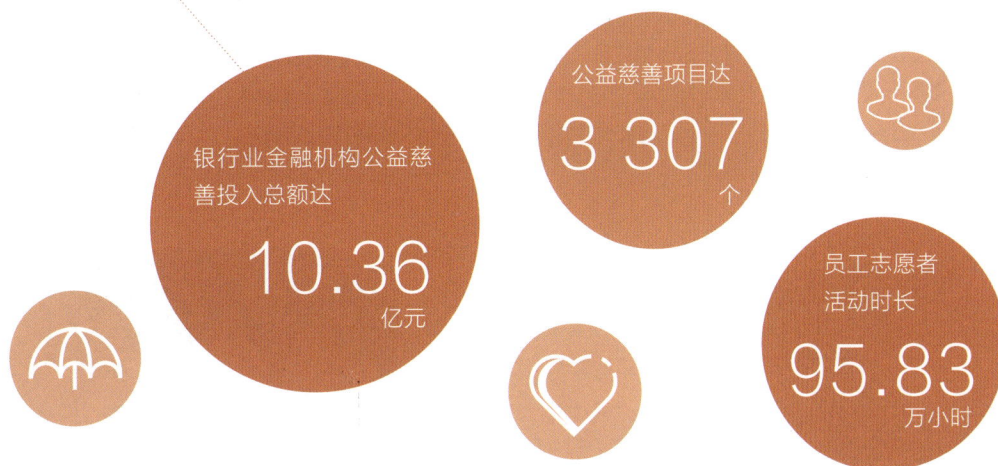

公益慈善项目达
3 307
个

银行业金融机构公益慈
善投入总额达
10.36
亿元

员工志愿者
活动时长
95.83
万小时

国家开发银行及政策性银行在扶贫、助老等领域开展公益项目，如国家开发银行参与的"黄手环行动"公益项目，研制了具有实时定位、双向通话、SOS 一键呼叫、安全围栏、历史轨迹查询等功能的第四代黄手环，帮助有走失倾向的老年人安全回家。

大型商业银行有效利用全球分支机构员工的集体力量，围绕助残关爱、绿色环保、捐资助学、公益宣教等主题，搭建社会公众参与平台，将公益行动与业务发展有机融合，打造具有金融特色的公益品牌。如中国农业银行持续开展"小积分·大梦想"公益行动，支持希望工程、关爱留守儿童和生态环保等公益事业；中国建设银行捐赠的"母亲健康快车"，在经济落后、交通不便的贫困山区，为村民提供健康咨询、义诊、孕产妇住院分娩免费接送、基层医务工作者培训以及特殊病例救助等服务。

股份制银行、城市商业银行、资产管理公司在推动公益发展中树立公益理念，形成公益慈善机制，并依托主营业务优势搭建和完善公益平台，设立公益基金、公益理财、慈善信托，引领社会各方力量开展助学、救灾、济困、助残、安老、扶幼等公益活动。

在股份制银行、资产管理公司等机构中涌现出一批如中国光大银行"母亲水窖"、广发银行"广发希望慈善基金"、平安银行"一路平安让爱回家"、招商银行"月捐悦多""小积分·微慈善"、上海浦东发展银行"爱与光明导盲犬支援计划"、兴业银行"美丽愿望献绿色爱心"、中国民生银行"我决定民生爱的力量——ME 公益创新资助计划"、浙商银行"爱心进大山"、中国信达资产管理公司"企业献关怀爱心到社区"、万向信托公司"善水基金信托"等系列特色公益实践。

在城市商业银行中，重庆银行开展"春暖重庆送爱回家"暨重庆银行返乡务工人员关爱行动；江苏银行持续发行"融梦想益家人"公益理财产品；深圳前海微众银行继续发挥"益点心意"项目的优势，让贫困地区校园的孩子吃上免费的午餐；广西北部湾银行、攀枝花商业银行、沧州银行等持续开展志愿者服务队相关公益活动。

农村商业银行、农村信用社联合社开展多元化公益实践。内蒙古自治区、江西、湖南、广西壮族自治区、辽宁、四川等农村信用社联合社积极推进志愿者服务活动；重庆农村商业银行开展智力助学活动，为涪陵区石坨镇石和乡小学贫困生带去希望和温暖；广州农村商业银行开展"太阳·无声的爱"听障儿童复听项目，让听障儿童重回有声的世界。

此外，一些外资银行通过设立公益基金、创立公益品牌平台、开展志愿者服务等实践支持公益事业发展。恒生银行（中国）创立"财智 YOUNG 学院"，培养青少年正确的财富观念，推动青少年的财商成长；三井住友银行（中国）开展"点点微光照亮你我"慈善义卖及探访活动等。

---

① 数据来源：中国银行业协会。

护航计划

"护航计划"是由中国儿童少年基金会发起的国家级大型公益项目,是集全国留学生登记系统、一站式服务平台与线下产业集群三位一体的留学全产业链生态系统和国家留学生保障工程。2017年,中信银行向"护航计划"捐赠 **1 000** 万元,同时向海外未成年留学生提供专属银行服务、文化认同养成服务和安全救援服务,使他们在安心求学的同时更具文化自觉和文化自信。

区块链技术·助力慈善公益事业

中国光大银行孵化用于"母亲水窖"公益慈善项目的区块链公益捐款系统,实现"母亲水窖"项目捐款信息公开、捐款费用可追溯、账务信息不可篡改及捐款者隐私保护,有效提升公益捐款透明度。

自2005年起,中国光大银行便与全国妇联、中国妇女发展基金会合作,倾力解决西部干旱缺水地区居民的饮水和用水难题。13年以来,累计捐款 **3 433** 万元,在甘肃、宁夏、内蒙古、陕西、广西、四川、青海、西藏、贵州、新疆、吉林、山西等 **12** 个省(区)捐建水窖 **8 593** 口,小型水利工程 **76** 处,校园安全饮水项目 **6** 处,为近 **13** 万名贫困地区群众解决饮水难题。

中国光大银行助力"母亲水窖"慈善事业

爱与光明·导盲犬支援计划

随着公众对于导盲犬了解的加深,它们的身影也在越来越多的地方被接纳。但我国导盲犬的普及程度远达不到国际导盲犬联盟规定的1%普及率。训练一只导盲犬需要2~3年,费用高达十几万元。

2017年12月,上海浦东发展银行携手私人银行客户持续推出公益理财产品,将到期时客户收益的一部分与浦发银行配捐以 **1:1** 的比例向大连慈善总会的"爱与光明导盲犬支援计划"捐赠。按产品规模 **10** 亿元估算,预估客户端捐赠 **37.5** 万元。

上海浦东发展银行发起"爱与光明——浦发银行导盲犬支援计划"

百善孝为先·平安在身边

平安银行连续四年在全国各地的分支机构策划举办了近百场形式多样的"百善孝为先·平安在身边"主题敬老活动,各营业厅举办健康养生讲座,为老年客户测量血压等;志愿者们还走进社区、敬老院探访老人,为老人们送上平安的关爱。该公益活动不仅为社会长者们送上平安银行的关爱与祝福,更是向全社会传递了尊老、敬老的理念。

平安银行开展"百善孝为先·平安在身边"主题敬老活动

慈善十年·希望足迹

2008 年，**广发银行**与中国青少年发展基金会共同成立"广发希望慈善基金"。十年来，该行与社会各界一道搭建慈善公益平台，汇聚社会资源，通过对教育助学、扶贫救助、疾病治疗等方面的善款投入，持续改善青少年的健康和教育条件，传递公益正能量。这十年，志愿者的脚步遍及了陕西、四川、甘肃、青海、新疆、云南、贵州、广西、宁夏、河南及湖北等区域的贫困地区。截至 2017 年底，"广发希望慈善基金"拥有员工志愿者 100 人，持卡人志愿者 50 人，志愿服务时长达 10 000 多个小时，共募集善款 7 520 万元，直接帮助 2.6 万多名大中小学生，改善了 15 万多名青少年的生活和学习环境。

中国建设银行举办"梦想起飞——建行希望夏令营"公益活动

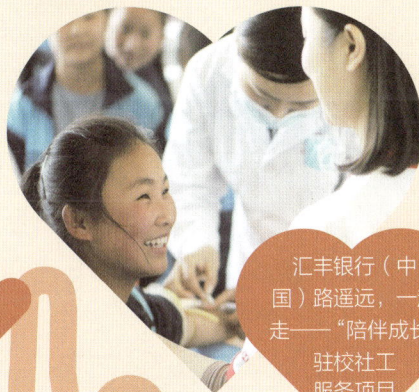

中国农业银行青年志愿者情系留守儿童共度快乐"六一"

澳大利亚和新西兰银行（中国）关爱自闭症儿童

汇丰银行（中国）路遥远，一起走——"陪伴成长"驻校社工服务项目

未来展望

2018 年，中国银行业金融机构要充分落实党的十九大精神，不忘初心，牢记使命，全面贯彻"创新、协调、绿色、开放、共享"的新发展理念，统筹资源，协调推进，致力于"深化供给侧结构性改革、实施乡村振兴战略、加快完善社会主义市场经济体制"，聚焦"服务实体经济，防控金融风险，深化金融改革"，在高质量发展的道路上不断砥砺前行。

服务实体经济。中国银行业金融机构要坚守本源，回归主业，主动适应经济发展新常态、把握新机遇，积极服务好供给侧结构性改革、加快助力"一带一路"建设，统筹发展"京津冀协调发展、雄安新区建设"等区域协调战略，不断增强创新能力，优化信贷结构，将信贷资源更多地投向新型产业、先进制造业和创新产业，提高经济发展的质量和效益。

致力普惠金融。中国银行业金融机构要积极贯彻落实党中央、国务院决策部署，大力支持小微企业、"三农"和精准脱贫等经济社会发展薄弱环节，着力解决融资难、融资贵问题，加快创新产品渠道，弥补服务短板，利用大数据、人工智能和云计算，精准客户画像，扩大普惠金融覆盖面，不断提升金融服务质效，开创普惠金融创新发展的新蓝海。

提供便捷服务。中国银行业金融机构要以"服务国家、服务社会、服务群众"为信条，深化服务管理体系建设，促进线上、线下多渠道互联互通，以"人工 + 智能"多位一体的服务模式，推进新型客户交互体验，以持续升级的金融服务满足用户全方位、多层次的金融消费需求，不断加强消费者权益保护，提升服务质效，改善客户体验。

推进绿色发展。中国银行业金融机构要时刻坚持绿水青山就是金山银山的绿色发展理念，不断建立健全绿色发展体系机制，发展绿色金融，壮大节能环保产业、清洁生产产业、清洁能源产业，加强绿色金融信息披露，加快创新绿色金融产品服务，解决好人与自然的和谐共生问题，助力生态文明建设再上新台阶。

促进社会和谐。中国银行业金融机构要深入开展脱贫攻坚，广泛投身于社会公益慈善事业中，推动共享经济发展，为人民带来美好生活；不断促进员工的全面发展，为员工营造健康成长的发展环境，提升员工幸福感。着力化解人民日益增长的美好生活需要与不平衡、不充分的发展现状之间的矛盾，为人民的美好生活、安居乐业提供保障。

2018 年，中国银行业金融机构要锐意进取，勇于变革，在全面建成小康社会的决胜阶段，更加紧密地团结在以习近平同志为核心的党中央周围，以高度的责任心、使命感、紧迫感，坚定信心，奋发作为，为实现中华民族伟大复兴的中国梦而努力奋斗。

附录

附录一　参与编写活动的主要金融机构名单

国家开发银行	绍兴银行	重庆农村商业银行
中国农业发展银行	台州银行	四川省农村信用社联合社
中国进出口银行	温州银行	甘肃省农村信用社联合社
中国工商银行	浙江稠州商业银行	大连农村商业银行
中国农业银行	浙江泰隆商业银行	徐州淮海农村商业银行
中国银行	徽商银行	厦门农村商业银行
中国建设银行	福建海峡银行	广州农村商业银行
交通银行	江西银行	汇丰银行（中国）
中国邮政储蓄银行	齐鲁银行	东亚银行（中国）
中信银行	德州银行	恒生银行（中国）
中国光大银行	焦作中旅银行	华侨永亨银行（中国）
华夏银行	广西北部湾银行	瑞穗银行（中国）
广发银行	桂林银行	三井住友银行（中国）
平安银行	海南银行	三菱东京日联银行（中国）
招商银行	重庆银行	玉山（中国）银行
上海浦东发展银行	乐山市商业银行	澳大利亚和新西兰银行（中国）
兴业银行	攀枝花商业银行	富邦华一银行
中国民生银行	雅安市商业银行	物产中大集团财务有限公司
恒丰银行	富滇银行	海亮集团财务有限责任公司
浙商银行	兰州银行	浙江省交通投资集团财务有限责任公司
渤海银行	青岛银行	海马财务有限公司
北京银行	深圳前海微众银行	杭银消费金融股份有限公司
河北银行	中国信达资产管理公司	杭州工商信托股份有限公司
保定银行	中国长城资产管理公司	万向信托有限公司
沧州银行	中央国债登记结算有限责任公司	中建投信托有限责任公司
邯郸银行	北京农商银行	浙商金汇信托股份有限公司
衡水银行	天津农村商业银行	大连保税区珠江村镇银行
丹东银行	内蒙古自治区农村信用社联合社	大连甘井子浦发村镇银行
哈尔滨银行	辽宁省农村信用社联合社	大连金州联丰村镇银行
上海银行	上海农商银行	大连旅顺口蒙银村镇银行
江苏银行	浙江省农村信用社联合社	大连庄河汇通村镇银行
苏州银行	江西省农村信用社联合社	荥阳利丰村镇银行
杭州银行	湖南省农村信用社联合社	海南澄迈长江村镇银行
嘉兴银行	广西壮族自治区农村信用社联合社	海南五指山长江村镇银行

中国银行业协会文件

银协发〔2018〕72号

关于表彰2017年中国银行业社会责任工作评估活动获奖先进机构及个人的决定

各会员单位：

2017 年，银行业积极贯彻落实全国金融工作会议和中央经济工作会议重要精神，紧跟经济发展新形势，以思维引领创新发展，以科技驱动经营转型，在风险防控、脱贫攻坚、服务"三农""小微"、推进绿色发展、加大对外开放等方面作出新贡献，实现了社会、经济、环境的协调发展。为持续推动中国银行业社会责任管理工作，引领会员单位将社会责任理念根植于企业文化，付诸于日常经营管理，中国银行业协会组织开展了 2017 年中国银行业社会责任工作评估活动。各会员单位高度重视、认真参与，全面梳理了 2017 年在社会责任工作上所做出的新突破，展示了银行业积极履行社会责任的良好精神面貌。

为保证评估活动公平、公开、公正，中国银行业协会邀请业内外社会责任管理专家，立足中国银行业社会责任工作实践，根据《2017 年中国银行业社会责任评估评分体系》和《2017 年中国银行业社会责任工作评估活动方案》，严格按照机构自评申报、参评资格审查、资料数据初评、专家测评复审、审议核定等工作流程，从管理绩效、经济绩效、环境绩效和社会绩效 4 个方面、12 个一级指标、79 个二级指标对参评单位及个人的社会责任管理工作做出全面评估。

为鼓励先进，树立榜样，中国银行业协会决定授予国家开发银行等 12 家会员单位"最具社会责任金融机构奖"；授予汇丰银行（中国）等 5 家会员单位"最佳公益慈善贡献奖"；授予浙商银行等 5 家会员单位"最佳民生金融奖"；授予兴业银行等 5 家会员单位"最佳绿色金融奖"；授予上海银行等 11 家会员单位"最佳社会责任实践案例奖"；授予中国工商银行新疆分行营业部党委委员、副总经理买买提依明·艾买提等 15 位同志"最佳社会责任管理者奖"；授予中国建设银行安康分行营业部等 18 家网点"年度最佳社会责任特殊贡献网点奖"。以上获奖单位及个人充分认识自身所肩负的社会责任，结合资源优势，在服务实体经济、推动综合金融发展、保护生态环境、优化客户服务体验及提升公益投入质效等领域发挥着重要作用，是银行业履行社会责任的优秀模范。

希望获得荣誉的单位和个人以身作则，严于利己，以更高标准督促自己开拓进取，充分发挥先进示范作用。同时，希望各会员单位加强经验交流，建立行业智库，携手攻克社会责任领域痛点、难点，为实现银行业可持续性健康发展贡献力量。

附件：2017 年中国银行业社会责任工作评估活动获奖先进机构及个人名单

2018 年 5 月 26 日

2017年中国银行业社会责任工作评估活动
获奖单位及个人名单

一、最具社会责任金融机构奖（12家）

国家开发银行、中国农业发展银行、中国进出口银行、中国工商银行、中国农业银行、中国银行、中国建设银行、交通银行、中国光大银行、招商银行、江苏银行、湖南省农村信用社联合社。

二、最佳公益慈善贡献奖（5家）

广发银行、中国民生银行、北京银行、重庆银行、汇丰银行（中国）。

三、最佳民生金融奖（5家）

中国邮政储蓄银行、华夏银行、浙商银行、杭州银行、内蒙古自治区农村信用社联合社。

四、最佳绿色金融奖（5家）

中信银行、兴业银行、上海浦东发展银行、青岛银行、重庆农村商业银行。

五、最佳社会责任实践案例奖（11家）

平安银行、上海银行、富滇银行、兰州银行、齐鲁银行、苏州银行、桂林银行、深圳前海微众银行、东亚银行（中国）、恒生银行（中国）、中国长城资产管理股份有限公司。

六、最佳社会责任管理者奖（15位）

国家开发银行江西省分行党委书记、行长 吴守华

中国工商银行新疆分行营业部党委委员、副总经理 买买提依明·艾买提

中国工商银行青海省分行海苑服务总公司办公室主任 乔小飞

中国工商银行达州分行党委委员 常艺腾

中国农业银行石渠县支行运营副主管 达瓦

中国农业银行河南兰考县支行"三农"业务中心"三农"客户经理 闫结实

中国银行广西壮族自治区驻村扶贫干部 覃毅敏

中国建设银行（亚洲）行长 江先周

中国建设银行绵阳分行党委委员、纪委书记、副行长 管建国

交通银行郑州百花路支行党总支书记、行长 刘放

中国邮政储蓄银行喀什地区分行党委书记、行长 郑建军

中信银行乌鲁木齐河北路支行行长助理 阿力甫·排孜加帕

兴业银行南京分行绿色金融部总经理 夏一飞

中国民生银行绍兴分行行长 王黎红

重庆农村商业银行武隆支行党委书记、行长 陈和平

七、最佳社会责任特殊贡献网点奖（18家）

国家开发银行甘肃省分行

中国进出口银行喀什分行

中国工商银行甘南分行营业室

中国工商银行通江支行

中国工商银行福州八一七支行营业室

中国农业银行加查县支行营业室

中国银行日喀则分行营业部

中国建设银行孟定支行

中国建设银行安康分行营业部

交通银行阿克苏分行营业部

中国邮政储蓄银行阿克陶县支行

平安银行珠海前山支行

兴业银行延边分行营业部

攀枝花市商业银行凉山分行营业部

固阳县农村信用合作联社红泥井信用社

德保市农村信用合作联社敬德信用社

重庆农村商业银行武隆支行

田东北部湾村镇银行

附录三 GRI 索引

		总体信息标准披露	
指标	序号	内容	索引位置
战略与分析	1	机构最高的决策者声明	采用
	2	主要影响、风险及机遇的描述	采用
机构概况	3	机构名称	采用
	4	主要品牌、产品和服务	采用
	6	机构在多少个国家运营，在哪些国家有主要业务，或哪些国家与报告所述的可持续发展事宜特别相关	采用
	8	机构所服务的市场（包括地区细分、所服务的行业、客户和受益人类型）	采用
	9	报告机构的规模，包括员工人数、运营地点数量、净销售额或净收入、按债务及权益细分的总市值、所提供的产品或服务的数量	采用
	10	根据雇佣合同和性别的分类报告员工总人数	未采用
	13	指出报告期当中关于机构的规模、结构、所有权或供应链的一切重大改变	未采用
	14	机构是否及如何按预警方针及原则行事	采用
	15	机构参与或支持的外界发起的经济、环境、社会公约、原则或其他倡议	采用
	16	机构加入的协会（行业协会）和全国或国际性倡议机构，并且在治理机构占有席位、参与项目或委员会、除定期缴纳会费外，提供大额资助、视成员资格具有战略意义	采用
	17	列出所有实体，包括机构的合并财务报表或与之相当的文件	未采用
	18	阐释确定报告内容和内容界限的过程	未采用
		阐释机构如何执行有关报告内容确定的报告原则	未采用
	19	列出报告内容确定过程中认定的所有重要方面	未采用
报告概况	28	所提供信息的报告期（如财政年度或日历年）	采用
	29	上一份报告的日期（如有）	采用
	30	报告周期	采用
	31	查询报告或报告内容的联络点	采用
	32	报告机构在两种可选标准中选择了哪一种	采用
		报告所选标准的 GRI 内容索引	采用
		如果报告采用了外部审验，指出在外部审验报告中的相应参考内容	未采用
	33	机构为报告寻求外部审验的政策和现行措施	未采用
		如未在可持续发展报告附带的审验报告中列出，则需解释已提供的任何外部审验的范围及根据	未采用
		说明报告机构与验证提供者之间的关系	未采用
最高管理机构在确定宗旨、价值和策略中的角色	42	报告最高管理机构和高层管理人员在发展、批准和更新机构的宗旨、价值或使命宣言、策略、政策和与经济、环境、社会影响相关的目标中的作用	采用
道德与诚信	56	描述机构的价值观、原则、标准和行为规范，例如行为准则和道德准则	采用
	57	披露机构寻求关于合规合法行为和廉正事宜建议的内外部机制，例如求助和咨询热线	采用

具体指标披露			
指标方面	序号	指标名称	索引
经济绩效	EC1	机构产生及分配的直接经济价值	未采用
	EC2	气候变化对机构活动产生的财务影响及其他风险和机遇	采用
	EC7	基础设施投资及支持服务的发展和影响	采用
	EC8	重大间接经济影响，包括影响的程度	采用
环境绩效	EN3	机构内部能源消耗	采用
	EN6	降低能源消耗	采用
	EN8	按源头说明总耗水量	未采用
	EN19	减少温室气体（GHG）排放	采用
	EN31	按类别说明总环保开支及投资	采用
劳工实践和体面工作	LA1	按年龄组别、性别及地区划分的新进员工和员工流失总数及比率	未采用
	LA8	与工会达成的正式协议中的健康与安全议题	采用
	LA9	按性别和员工类别划分，每名员工每年接受培训的平均时数	采用
	LA10	加强员工持续就业能力及协助员工转职的技能管理及终生学习计划	采用
	LA11	按性别和员工类别划分，接受定期绩效及职业发展考评的员工的百分比	未采用
	LA12	按性别、年龄组别、少数族裔成员及其他多元化指标划分，治理机构成员和各类员工的组成	未采用
当地社区	SO1	实施了当地社区参与、影响评估和发展计划的运营点比例	采用
	SO4	关于反腐败政策及程序的交流与培训	采用
	SO6	按国家以及受援方说明，政治捐献的总值	采用
产品责任	PR3	机构产品、服务信息和标识程序要求的产品和服务信息种类，以及需要标明这种信息的重要产品和服务的百分比	采用
	PR5	客户满意度调查结果	未采用

Realistically Exercising the Concepts of Social Responsibilities

"In order to implement the relevant policy of the Party and the State, and to respond to the new expectations of the public on the banking sector, the banking industry should hold its social responsibility from the levels of corporate culture, mission, actions in three main intentions, with concerted efforts as a joint community. The first is to serve the real economy, the second is to win the trust of the public, and the third is to pursue the management of responsibility. "

——Pan Guangwei, Party Secretary and CEO of China Banking Association

"Banking financial institutions should prioritize their main businesses to focus on the businesses with real potentials, strengthen the ability of serving the real economy, depress the center of gravity, vigorously develop inclusive finance, steadily expand the coverage of basic finance, deepen the concept of responsibility, continuously enhance their ability to carry out their duties; strengthen industry self-discipline and actively promote the concept and culture of banking responsibility. "

——Mei Zhixiang, director of department of Public Relations of China Banking and Insurance Regulatory Commission

"In the face of the new situation, banking financial institutions should focus on supporting national strategies to meet the needs of financial services in key areas of the country; promote 'responsible' financial development and promote healthy and sustainable economic and social development; and pay attention to building responsible brands, so as to achieve its own strong and sustainable development. "

——Zhang Qingsong, Vice Governor of Bank of China and Representative of the Seventh Chairman Unit of China Banking Association

"The social responsibility is an eternal task. We should be committed to work for the mission as a member of the community, and strive to act with a clear purpose. Banking financial institutions and related departments should continue to explore and carry out work step-by-step in accordance with regulatory requirements and industry standards. Begin with every individuals, progress bit by bit based on the practical industrial environment, when establishing systems and mechanisms, and allocating financial material and human resource, continue to strengthen and improve the system of social responsibility management, adapt to the requirements of the new era, adhere to innovation drive, constantly enrich the way of social responsibility management, so as to support the national strategic development and enhance the ability of sustainable development of enterprises. "

——Huang Runzhong, Secretary General of China Banking Association

In 2017, the banking financial institutions have implemented the requirements of "strong supervision", exercised the concept of responsibility in a practical manner, and practically served the development of the real economy, firmly implemented the bottom-line thinking, firmly adhered to the "bottom line without systemic financial risks"; focused on and protected the main business, actively served the supply-side structural reform, actively carried out innovation, strengthened the awareness of risk prevention, and deepened cooperation among the same industry. The institutions have vigorously supported the development of the country's opening up to the outside world; sought new ideas pragmatically, focused on the difficult points, improved the level of specialization and refinement of financial services, and implemented the strategy of making a strong country. The institutions have further developed the key role of inclusive finance and green finance in poverty eradication, agricultural sustainability and environmental protection.

Deepen stakeholder participation mechanisms. Banking financial institutions have deeply promoted multi-party cooperation, helped to carry out national strategies, "Belt and Road Initiative" included, promoted industrial transformation and upgrading, upgraded financial services for agriculture, rural areas and farmers, supported the development of small and micro enterprises, and promoted green development. By giving full play to the advantages of all parties and optimizing the risk boundary of all parties, the institutions realized economic benefits and take into account social and environmental benefits, and devoted themselves to promoting the coordinated and sustainable development of economy, society and environment.

Strengthen communication and cooperation. The banking financial institutions have deepened exchanges with their international and domestic counterparts and participated in activities related to social responsibility such as the United Nations Global Compact, the United Nations Environment Program, the Global Reporting Initiative (GRI) and the Equator Principles (EP), shared and exchanged experiences of responsibility management and practice, and understood the latest trends of social responsibility development. At the same time, in the process of increasing business cooperation and business promotion, the institutions have strengthened the sharing of the concept of responsibility consensus and sustainable competitiveness, and constantly created a good ecological environment for the healthy and sustainable development of the banking industry.

Promote the development of social responsibility work in depth. A seminar on social responsibility in China's banking sector was held in Beijing in 2017. With the theme of "ramming up the consensus on responsibility and contributing to the sustainable development of banking", the experts in relevant area have shared their experiences. The experience sharing covered four themes, namely, "the design and promotion of social responsibility management systems," "sustainable development management based on sustainable development strategies," "product and service innovation to address environmental challenges and social needs," "the excellent projects executed based on the concept of social responsibility and the way of conduction." The seminar on social responsibility has become a platform for banking financial institutions to share and exchange ideas in social responsibility management, and has been gradually solidified into an annual meeting, which lays a foundation for deepening the consensus on the responsibility of member banks, enhancing the reputation of the industry, promoting the trust of the public to the banking industry and establishing a good social ecology for the sustainable development of the banking industry.

2017 is the tenth consecutive year that China Banking Association has released the "China Banking Social Responsibility report". The basic goal of the report is to set up a long-term propulsion mechanism of banking accountability and improve the practical level of banking performance management, to provide a platform for the industry to demonstrate and exchange social responsibility management experience, research on management practice and test and evaluate the performance, as well as to condense industry consensus, stimulate internal motivation, display the image of responsibility, and continuously enhance the impact of industry responsibility.

Safeguarding the Baseline, Preventing and Controlling Financial Risks

Banking financial institutions have thoroughly implemented the general requirement of "putting prevention and control of financial risks in a more important position" "from the Central Economic Work Conference. In accordance with the principles of returning to the source, focusing on the main business, and lowering the center of gravity, the institutions have taken "serving the national strategy and maintaining the safety of state-owned assets" as the main task, established scientific development concept and strategic direction, continuously strengthened compliance risk management, strengthened the construction of governance systems (i.e. the systems of decision-making, implementation, supervision and evaluation, etc), focused on key areas of risk resolution, multi-measures to improve the effectiveness of risk management and control, firmly guarded the baseline of "no systemic financial risks."

Banking financial institutions have effectively increased their awareness of racing against risk and running ahead of risks, and have highlighted risk control in key areas (i.e. market risk, credit risk, interest rate risk, reputation risk, operational risk, scientific and technological risk, etc), strengthened risk management covering the whole process, all functions and all business sectors, carried out various kinds of audit, investigation and evaluation, improved the accuracy of risk monitoring, warning and risk control in key areas, and improved the overall risk management responsibility system comprehensively, so as to maintain the continued and steady development.

Based on the principle of "risk as the base and compliance goes first", banking financial institutions have actively and effectively controlled the risk of money laundering and terrorist financing, and adopted measures such as perfecting the processing procedures by system, innovating the working pattern of monitoring, screening and reporting money laundering risks, so as to establish anti-money-laundering filter step by step. The institutions have consistently implemented the spirit of the eight stipulations of the Central Committee, by innovating the supervisory mechanism, comprehensively performing supervisory duties, improving the construction of a style of work and culture, and fighting against corruption in a realistic manner, and building a clean government. The institutions have also further improved the ability of discrimination, self-control and awareness of employees, constantly optimized the internal control environment, improved the internal control system, created a good compliance culture, strengthened compliance risk monitoring and analysis, and provided a solid guarantee for the steady operation of the banking industry.

▶ Banks in Action

China Development Bank has integrated the Basel Accord concept and method into risk management practice, deepened the construction of credit risk internal rating system, established and perfected the management system of market risk internal model method and operational risk management system and evaluated the use of "economic capital" in performance appraisal and portfolio management. All of these have formed a unique, effective and comprehensive risk management system and long-term credit risk management method, which provided a strong guarantee for the steady development of business.

Agricultural Development Bank of China has strengthened communication and exchanges, fully grasped the difficulties and key issues in the overall risk management, conducted special discussions around the contents of capital management, overall risk management, RWA system construction, and analyzed the consulting service needs on the building of a comprehensive risk management system. The bank has actively cooperated with external consulting organizations, formally set up a consulting project team, reviewed and evaluated the existing management system of the bank, so as to create Variance Analysis reports and improvement programs.

Agricultural Bank of China has optimized the organization structure of anti-money laundering, set up anti-money laundering centers in the head office and first-level branches, and centralized the anti-money laundering monitoring and analysis business. The bank has formulated special systems for the management of large-scale transactions and suspicious transaction reports, and measures for the freezing of assets involved in terrorist activities, and improved the system of anti-money laundering.

Bank of China and an internet company have launched the "new generation of online financial risk control system". The new generation of system has fully introduced the leading technologies in big data, cloud computing, machine learning from the internet companies on the foundation of the bank's overall risk control system to monitor financial activities in due-course, which provided users-convenient Internet financial services, a comprehensive, full process, real-time and efficient anti-fraud services. Such services have ensured the security of users' deposits and accounts, with the "duel-upgrade" of risk prevention and control as well as customer experience.

Huaxia Bank has improved its working mechanism, upgraded its anti-money laundering information system, strengthened the management of high-risk operations, and comprehensively improved the quality and effectiveness of anti-money laundering management. In 2017, the bank has launched a new generation of anti-money laundering system, becoming one of the joint-stock commercial banks to submit anti-money laundering data in accordance with No. 3 Decree of the People's Bank of China (2016). Throughout the year, it has actively cooperated with the regulatory authorities and the competent organs to carry out cooperative inspections and distribution and control work for more than 50 times.

Industrial Bank has strengthened risk compliance management, conscientiously implemented the requirements of "three violations", "three arbitrage" and "four improper special treatment and "market chaos" rectification work, and taken the initiative to carry out "blanket" risk investigation throughout the group, persisted in carrying out the reform while checking and building up, effectively identified the loopholes and guarded against risks, carried out the campaign of compliance & internal control, and a comprehensive competition and training project, which greatly enhanced staff risk awareness.

Bank of Beijing has established a risk reporting mechanism, held regular risk reporting meetings of investment institutions, and fully grasped the situation of risk prevention and control of subsidiary organizations in a timely manner, and established a mechanism for inspection, notification, rectification and supervision, and through inspection, rectification and reform, the bank has continued to standardize and improve the work of risk management in subsidiary organizations.

Hang Seng Bank (China) has launched its new anti-money laundering transaction monitoring system. At the same time, considering the business characteristics, customer group characteristics, trading habits and other factors, combining the data required for suspicious activity monitoring model and the feasibility of internal data extraction, the bank has discontinued the former 18 suspicious transaction monitoring rules, and formed a system that integrated central data of the bank and local autonomous monitoring model.

Keeping the Mission of Serving the Real Economy in Mind

(1) Serving Supply-side Structural Reform

(2) Supporting Coordinated Regional Development

(3) Accelerating China's Opening up to the World

(4) Promoting the Innovation-driven Development

Banking financial institutions have firmly adhered to the principles of serving the real economy, preventing and controlling financial risks, deepening the key tasks of financial reform, sticking to the source and focusing on the main business, actively participated in the supply-side structural reform, implemented regional strategies including "Belt and Road Initiative" construction, coordinated development between Beijing, Tianjin and Hebei, and the Yangtze Economic belt construction, deepened financial reform, enhanced comprehensive financial service capacity, and promoted the development of opening to the outside world. For the "made in China 2025", the banking financial institutions have put in efforts to strengthen supports for the transformation and upgrading of the manufacturing industry, constantly improved the quality and efficiency of the real economy, and promoted the development of high-quality real economy.

In 2017[1]

Aggregate Financing to the Real Economy(stock) had reached RMB **174 710** billion

presenting a YoY increase of **12%**

among which the balance of RMB loans to the real economy had reached RMB **119 030** billion

with a YoY increase of **13.2%**

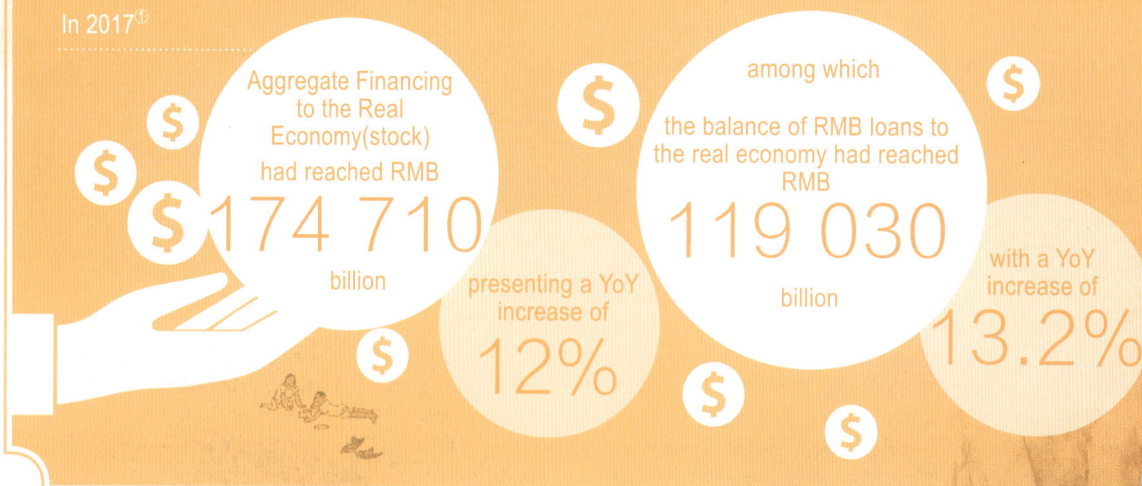

[1] Data source: The People's Bank of China.

(1) Serving Supply-side Structural Reform

Banking financial institutions have actively participated in the supply-side structural reform, around five prior principles of "cutting overcapacity, reducing inventory, deleveraging, lowering costs, and strengthening areas of weakness", deepened reform, actively innovated, continued to accelerate the optimization and upgrading of "zombie enterprises", and reduction of the over-capacity. The institutions have developed market-oriented legalized debt-for-equity swap, actively and steadily reduced leverage, implemented differential housing credit policy, resolutely curbed the real estate market bubble in some regions, by facilitating the destocking of housing. The institutions have strengthened management of service charges and increased financial supply, which effectively reduced enterprise costs; further strengthened services on the weak links of agricultural sector and small and micro enterprises, and provided services to support various new business sectors and new energy sectors, and actively supported the construction of "Belt and Road Initiative", provided more effective financial services for enterprises to "go abroad" and "bring in new projects"; vigorously promoted the construction of a green financial system, improved green financial products and services, strengthened social and environmental risk management, and promoted the "coordinated and sustainable development of the economic, social and environmental environment".

▶ Banks in Action

Support to reduce overcapacity

China Development Bank, Industrial and Commercial Bank of China, Bank of Communications, and other large commercial banks have strictly implemented national industrial policies and the policy requirement of "reducing over-productivity", carefully selected projects to support and control, provided financial services, and implemented differentiated and refined industry credit policies. The banks have drafted individual plans for enterprises from iron and steel, coal and papermaking industries; at the same time, the banks have taken the initiative to support advanced equipment manufacturing and high-tech industries with new business patterns and new models, developing areas with new economic growth potentials so as to accelerate the economic transformation.

In 2017, the balance of loans in excess capacity sectors of China Development Bank decreased by RMB66.2 billion compared with the beginning of the year, while Agricultural Bank of China reduced RMB181.4 billion of creditprovided to the 13 overcapacity industries, such as steel and coal, and other high risk industries. The loan balance of China Construction Bank on overcapacity sectors fell by RMB7.92 billion compared with the previous year, while loan balance for the serious overcapacity sector of Bank of Communications fell 0.7 percentage point compared with the beginning of the year.

Facilitate the deleveraging process

In September 2017, ICBC Financial Asset Investment Corporation has been launched with the purpose to help enterprises reduce leverage, promote corporate capital reduction, deepen reform, and tailor-make a debt-equity conversion program to enhance capital strength and governance efficiency.

China Construction Bank has maintained the advantage of the market-oriented debt-to-equity, successfully converted debt amount of RMB589.7 billion and an amount of RMB100.8 billion from the landing projects, which greatly helped the deleveraging.

Bank of Communications has designed relevant business models and service schemes to guide business units at all levels to "deleveraging" in a variety of ways. By the end of 2017, 11 projects of the market-oriented debt-to-equity conversion agreement under the framework had been signed, with the amount of RMB120 billion.

With full consideration of the leveraging needs of different industries and enterprises, using the debt financing tools, equity pledge financing, industry guidance funds and other direct financing methods, Industrial Bank has promoted non-financial enterprises to increase the proportion of direct financing, and actively paid close attention to and prudently promote the debt-equity conversion pilot, which effectively helped enterprises to deleverage.

Facilitate the destocking

China Development bank, as the main source of funding, has deployed differentiated operations according to the needs, provided loans for households' relocation of shanty housing redevelopment projects, actively supported the shanty housing redevelopment projects, and accelerated the development of rental housing pilot projects. By the end of 2017, loan balance provided to shanty housing projects had accumulated to RMB3.41 trillion to more than 20 million households, of which RMB880 billion was awarded within one year.

Agricultural Bank of China has implemented the relevant requirements of the state to speed up the establishment of a rental and purchase housing system and actively supported the development of rental housing business in large and medium-sized cities where the population flows into large and medium-sized cities.

China Construction Bank has prompted to land the "encourage both housing purchase and renting" policy in China. Comprehensive Housing rental solution took place in pilot cities like Foshan, Guangdong and Shenzhen.

Facilitate the cost reduction

Industrial and Commercial Bank of China has taken the initiative to adapt to the trend of financial disintermediation and deleveraging for enterprises, actively supported enterprises to issue various kinds of bonds in the interbank market to help enterprises reduce their financing costs. By the end of 2017, the bank had issued more than RMB4 trillion of bonds and invested about RMB4 trillion in various types of renminbi bonds.

China ZheShang Bank has continued to promote the iterative innovation of pool financing business. Through the three platforms of "pool financing", "Yi enterprise bank" and "chained receivable", the bank has provided comprehensive financial service schemes for the real economy, and made the current assets of enterprises to help reduce costs and increase efficiency. By the end of 2017, the "Yingjin" series of pooled products had helped customers save interest expenses of RMB1.69 billion.

Through the operation mechanism of the creditors' committee, Bank of Qingdao has adopted the methods of lowering the interest rate on loans, waived the unpaid interest rates, adjusted the repayment period and the frequency of interest repayment, so as to effectively help enterprises in temporary difficulties to achieve industrial transformation and upgrading and reduce financing costs.

China Development Bank has actively implemented services to support regional development strategies such as "Belt and Road Initiative", the coordinated development of Beijing, Tianjin and Hebei, and in particular the construction of the Xiong'an New area. The bank has continued to increase support for the allocation of financial resources in the areas of poverty alleviation, government-subsidized housing, scientific and technological innovation, ecological protection, education and medical care.

Agricultural Development Bank of China and Agricultural Bank of China, under the guidance of the strategy of rural revitalization, have played an important role in implementing the supply-side structural reform of agriculture and supporting the modernization of agricultural rural areas.

Large commercial banks have actively linked up with major regional and national strategies such as "Belt and Road Initiative" and "becoming a powerful manufacturing countries", established and improved inclusive financial organization mechanisms, and increased financial support to weak links such as small and micro enterprises, three rural areas" and poverty alleviation, and improved the green financial system for further green development.

Postal Savings Bank of China has practically explored the new rules, new mechanisms and new characteristics of China's inclusive finance in the new era, fully exerted its advantages on network, capital and professional expertise, constructed an ecological circle of community financial services, and helped in support of "three rural areas", the small and micro development and poverty alleviation.

Joint-stock banks have continuously increased the financial services for "Belt and Road Initiative", deepened the innovation of science, technology and finance, supported the "four new" economy of new technologies, new products, new forms of business and new models, and vigorously implemented inclusive finance, further analyzed the financing difficulties of small and micro enterprises, made effective use of Fintech and emerging technologies to support the development of small and micro enterprises, and increased green financial innovation, environmental friendliness and ecological civilization.

City commercial banks, rural commercial banks, rural credit cooperatives and village banks have implemented the agricultural supply-side structural reform policies, in-depth integration of the actual and industrial characteristics of the region, provided "three rural issues" with comprehensive quality services; actively practiced double-innovation, multi-measures to support the development of small and micro enterprises.

Asset management companies have provided Chinese enterprises with customized, specialized and differentiated financial solutions in order to exercise international cooperation and infrastructure construction in countries along route of "Belt and Road Initiative", and supported agricultural modernization and intensive development projects, assisted the agricultural and food safety.

Foreign banks have continued to serve the construction of "Belt and Road Initiative", increased the support to "three rural areas", small and micro businesses, and promoted sustainable finance.

Support weak-links

(2) Supporting Coordinated Regional Development

Banking financial institutions have carried out in-depth arrangements of the Party Central Committee and the State Council on regional development strategies, fully and rationally allocated financial resources, deepened comprehensive financial services, by offloading non-capital functions of Beijing, promoting the coordinated development of Beijing, Tianjin and Hebei, constructing Xiong'an New Area with high specifications and high level starting point, supporting the Yangtze River Economic Zone with the green economy innovation drives. The institutions continue to boost the development of central region, support the eastern region to take the lead, and help revitalize the old industrial bases in the Northeast.

Support the Development of the Xiong'an New Area

China Development Bank, policy banks and Bank of China and other large commercial banks have taken the initiative to link up with the major national deployment for Xiong'an New area, strengthened organizational leadership, formulated investment and financing plans, accurately met the needs of the new areas, and actively served the construction of the new areas. Large commercial banks have made use of diversified service channels to support the construction of Xiong'an New Area's infrastructure, industrial financing, ecological environment, and small towns with special features, and continued to improve the financial service capacity of the new district. By the end of 2017, China Development Bank had completed a pre-grant credit of RMB177.4 billion for the initial area collection and resettlement project; Agricultural Development Bank of China has approved two projects supporting the construction of the Xiong'an New Area, with a quota of RMB80.9 billion and a forestry loan project, the balance of the loan was RMB125 million; Bank of China has provided RMB22 billion special credit to the new area for demolition and relocation compensation.

Support the Coordinated development of Beijing, Tianjin and Hebei

Policy banks, Industrial and Commercial Banks of China, Agricultural Bank of China, Bank of China, and other large commercial banks, have focused on the coordinated development of the national strategy between Beijing, Tianjin and Hebei, applied comprehensive means of financial services to speed up the innovation of financial products and services. The banks have focused on providing financial support for major projects and livelihood projects such as the Beijing-Tianjin-Hebei track, highways, ecological construction, non-capital functions offloading, industrial upgrading and transferring and livelihood projects, so as to promote complementary advantages, industrial upgrading and innovative development of Beijing-Tianjin-Hebei. By the end of 2017, Agricultural Development Bank of China had supported 36 forestry projects in Tianjin and Hebei, handled loan application of RMB23.55 billion and approved RMB11.61 billion of loans. Agricultural Bank of China had granted RMB485.1 billion of credit to customers in the field of Beijing-Tianjin-Hebei cooperative development. Bank of China had supported 418 cooperative development projects in Beijing, Tianjin and Hebei, with a loan balance of RMB277.2 billion.

Support the Construction of the Yangtze Economic Belt

Policy banks, large commercial banks such as Bank of China and joint-stock banks such as Industrial Bank have continued to innovate financial services, optimized the allocation of credit resources, and actively practiced green finance, helped optimize and upgrade the industrial structure along the Yangtze River, protect and rationally utilize the Yangtze River water resources, implemented projects such as the ecological environment of the Yangtze River, the construction of new urbanization and infrastructure construction, and contributed to the construction of the Yangtze River Economic Belt. Industrial Bank Financial Leasing Company, Industrial Bank's wholly owned subsidiary, has participated in the strategic alliance of serving the Yangtze Economic Belt by providing leasing service, the strategic cooperation agreement signed between the alliance and the Development and Reform Commission of 11 provinces and cities will provide no less than 300 billion of intended leasing supporting green ecological corridor of the Yangtze River, standardization of ship type, comprehensive three-dimensional transportation, industrial transformation and upgrading, new type of urbanization, etc. By the end of 2017, Bank of China had added RMB66.38 billion of credit to the "Yangtze River Economic Belt" project, with a credit balance of RMB26.84 billion for the whole year. The loan balance in the Yangtze River Economic Zone of Postal Savings Bank of China had amounted to RMB310.065 billion.

Support the development of central and western regions

Policy banks such as Agricultural Development Bank of China, large commercial banks such as Agricultural Bank of China, Postal Savings Bank of China, joint-stock banks such as China CITIC Bank, City banks such as Chongqing Bank, have increased their efforts to extend credit to the western region. The institutions have set up a new type of urban fund, optimized the structure of regional economic loans, actively supported infrastructure construction and the development of specialized industries, promoted the transformation of énterprises, and made every effort to support the high-quality growth of the economy in the central and western regions and the transformation and development of the economic structure. By the end of 2017, the balance of loans in the western region of Agricultural Bank of China had amounted to RMB2.41 trillion, while that of Postal Savings Bank of China in the western development area had reached RMB189.70 billion, and that of the western region of China CITIC Bank had totaled RMB389.15 billion.

Agricultural Development Bank of China supported the "co-development of two districts" project for the overall urbanization of Xiyong at Shapingba district in Chongqing.

ICBC invested and offered loans to Guiyang rail transit PPP project

China Merchants Bank supported Highway Construction in Western China

Support the revitalization of Northeast Old Industrial Base

China Development Bank has signed the Agreement on Joint Promotion of the Strategic Cooperation for the Revitalization of the Old Industrial Bases in Northeast China with State Development and Reform Commission, and jointly launched the "Northeast Revitalizing Financial Cooperation Scheme" with more than 40 financial institutions. Bank of Communications and other large commercial banks have actively supported major fields and weak links such as infrastructure construction, industrial upgrading, rundown urban area in Northeast of China. Postal Savings Bank of China focused on supporting projects such as highway, airport construction, wind power development and railway construction in the old industrial areas of Northeast of China. By the end of 2017, the balance of loans in the northeastern region had amounted to RMB43.21 billion.

Banking financial institutions such as Harbin Bank, Liaoning Rural Credit Cooperatives have promoted the establishment of resource-based cities, continuously improved financial services, innovated credit models, and increased the intensity of credit investment, which supported the supply-side structural reform and inclusive financial construction in Northeast of China.

(3) Accelerating China's Opening up to the World

Banking financial institutions took the initiative to adapt to the new situation of opening up to the world, coordinated and accelerated the top-level planning of serving "Belt and Road Initiative" service, continuously upgraded the capacity of cross-border financing, and formulated a number of credit policies and measures. Through a variety of financial instruments, such as syndicated loans, contracted project loans, mutual loans, and so on, the banking institutions have reasonably steered credit supply, carried out business innovation, system innovation and management innovation, and provided diversified financial services to Chinese and foreign enterprises. In addition, the banking financial institutions have actively taken precautions against the risks of "B&R projects", deepened cooperation with the national financial industry involved in "Belt and Road Initiative", participated in the construction of financial infrastructure, and provided a financial engine for the development of comprehensive service opening to the outside world.

China development banks and policy banks have played an important role in optimizing bilateral and multilateral cooperation, providing investment and financing support, and promoting enterprises and industries to "go out" and "bring in". Industrial and Commercial Bank of China, Bank of China and other large commercial banks have actively improved the global service network and actively adapted to the diversified financial service needs of customers. Through a series of product combinations such as cross-border M & A loans, cross-border capital pools and direct loans abroad, enterprises have been encouraged to "go abroad"; joint-stock banks and city commercial banks have constantly increased their reserves of high-quality credit projects and created a platform for financing, payment and settlement at home and abroad, providing customers with comprehensive financial solutions. By the end of 2017, 10 Chinese banks had set up 68 first-level institutions in 26 countries along the "Belt and Road", and a total of 1,013 foreign banks had been operating in China with a total asset of RMB3.24 trillion.[1]

Expand the global operation

By the end of 2017, Industrial and Commercial Bank of China had set up 419 institutions in 45 countries and regions around the world, indirectly covering 20 sub-Saharan African countries through its stake in the South African Standard Bank Group. The bank has established agency relations with 1,545 foreign institutions in 143 countries and regions, 1,371 of which are at the head office level of China Construction Bank, covering 132 countries and regions, and basically covering countries along "Belt and Road". Bank of Communications has established agency relations with 515 banks in 55 countries along the route of "Belt and Road Initiative", and Postal Savings Bank of China has set up a total of 997 agencies, including 40 "Belt and Road Initiative" countries and 240 banks. The amount of agencies along the routes of "Belt and Road Initiative" of Huaxia Bank was 739.

Deepen the construction of free trade zones

Bank of China has been increasing its support for the construction of a free trade zone in Shanghai. By the end of 2017, the bank had opened more than 15,000 free trade accounts and funded RMB13 billion for cross-border loans, helped thousands of enterprises to develop rapidly within the zone. Shanghai Pudong Development Bank has actively implemented the financial support policy of the Shanghai Free Trade Zone, devoted itself to supporting the construction of the Science and Technology Center, further expanding the FT account function, expanding the cross-border use of RMB, and building an international financial factor market. Based on serving the Hong Kong and Macao regions, China Guangfa Bank has helped to build Guangdong-Hong Kong-Macau Greater Bay Area and promoted the construction of the Qianhai, Nansha and Hengqin free trade pilot areas. Bank of Shanghai has fully integrated and utilized domestic and foreign resources and innovated policies in the free trade zone, and built a cross-border financial services platform to support the construction of Shanghai Technological Innovation Center and free trade port.

Provide service of international settlement

By the end of 2017, Agricultural Development Bank of China had handled RMB3.15 billion of cross-border renminbi transactions; Bank of China had handled RMB3.83 trillion of international settlement; China Construction Bank's international settlement volume had reached USD 1.17 trillion, and cross-border RMB settlement at home and abroad amounted to RMB2.05 trillion. Bank of Communications had handled RMB2 trillion of cross-border RMB settlement; China Everbright Bank had handled 11,398 cross-border RMB settlement transactions with a total amount of RMB24.91 billion; Shanghai Pudong Development Bank had handled more than RMB450 billion in cross-border RMB settlement.

Support enterprises to "go abroad"

By the end of 2017, The Export-Import Bank of China had 1,448 "Belt and Road Initiative" credit projects, had opened offices/branches in more than 50 countries along the route, had provided loan of more than RMB700 billion. Industrial and Commercial Bank of China had supported 358 projects with the total amount of loans reaching USD94.5 billion; Bank of China had accumulated about 4,205 projects supporting "going abroad" projects, with loan commitments exceeding USD280.5 billion; China Construction Bank had accumulated 268 major projects in more than 50 countries and regions along the routes of "Belt and Road Initiative", with the investment amount of USD466 billion.

Guard against financial risks

The Export-Import Bank of China has strengthened its dynamic monitoring over country-risks and carried out quantitative country risk monitoring and quantitative management in ten "Belt and Road Initiative" countries, including Pakistan, Cambodia and Laos, and etc. Industrial and Commercial Bank of China has actively supported the "Belt and Road Initiative" to serve the economic and trade and investment projects of Chinese enterprises in countries along the route of B&R, through a series of product portfolios such as cross-border M & A loans, cross-border capital pools, direct overseas loans, risk reference loans, internal and external loans, etc.; Agricultural Bank of China has set up special funds for "going out" to perfect the relevant system of "going abroad". In the process of pursuing "Belt and Road Initiative", Huaxia Bank has strengthened the management of the credit risk, country risk, environment and social risk of cross-border business. Aiming at the difficult points of the international settlement business of foreign trade enterprises in the "Belt and Road" region, such as complicated business procedure and long period of cycle, China Guangfa Bank has innovated and introduced a series of products called "Cross-border instantaneous Communication", so as to truly realize the full-process paperless service for import and export business, which has greatly improved the efficiency of international settlement for businesses, and effectively prevented the risk of trade fraud.

[1] Data source:China Banking and Insurance Regulatory Commission.

ICBC supported a Chinese shipyard to build the world's largest ore tanker which will be used for the transportation of ore between Brazil and China.

▶ Banks in Action

Communication and Cooperation

China Development Bank has organized the Eurasian Economic Forum on Financial Cooperation, the third Forum on Investment in Africa, the annual meeting of the BRICS Bank Cooperation Mechanism, the Seventh China-ASEAN UnionPay Conference and the Infrastructure Connectivity Financial Forum, China-Australia CEO Round Table, 18th International Advisory Council, Shanghai Cooperation Organization UnionPay Symposium and other international conferences. The establishment of the China-CEE UnionPay, jointly with 13 financial institutions in Central and Eastern Europe, aimed at more rational and effective integration of financial resources through the establishment of a new type of multilateral financial cooperation mechanism under the "16 + 1 cooperation" mechanism which Jointly provided long-term and effective investment and financing support for major projects in the region to promote the sustainable economic and social development of China-Central and Eastern European countries.

As a member of the Preparatory Committee for the "Belt and Road Initiative" Summit Forum on International Cooperation, The Export-Import Bank of China has closely cooperated with the relevant ministries and departments and actively participated in the holding of the Forum. In the summit forum's list of results, the bank has signed 28 loan agreements, totaling about RMB42.5 billion, covering transportation, electricity, communications, equipment manufacturing, international production capacity and financial cooperation. A special loan quota of RMB equivalent of RMB130 billion has been set up to support the infrastructure construction, production capacity and financial cooperation of "Belt and Road Initiative".

Industrial and Commercial Bank of China has held a round-table meeting of bankers to form the Beijing Joint statement of B&R Bankers Round Table, which proposed to establish the normal cooperation mechanism between B&R banks, based on the concept of mechanism co-construction, benefit-sharing, responsibility-sharing and win-win cooperation. Bank of China has followed the National Framework Agreement on deepening Cooperation between Guangdong, Hong Kong and Macao to promote the Construction of the Dawan District, set up an organizational mechanism to support the development of Guangdong-Hong Kong-Macau Greater Bay Area, and set up the "Guangdong, Hong Kong and Macao Cooperation Development Committee" to promote the business linkage between Guangdong, Hong Kong and Macao institutions, and accelerate the realization of inter-regional customer integration services and information systems interconnection, to assist the construction of Guangdong-Hong Kong-Macau Greater Bay Area.

China Merchants Bank has held a "Belt and Road Offshore Financial Services Symposium", inviting dozens of Chinese enterprises doing overseas investment and contracting to explore the financial services needs and solutions in the pursuing of "Belt and Road Initiative". In 2017, the bank has cooperated with 40 related enterprises in overseas project financing, involving Indonesia, Bangladesh, Vietnam, Zambia and other countries along the routes of "Belt and Road Initiative".

In response to the "Belt and Road Initiative", Bank of Communications has deepened financial cooperation with ASEAN countries including Cambodia, and successfully completed the renminbi's initial exchange with Cambodia's Rier. The photo shows the launching ceremony of RMB regional trading in the RuierInterbank Market in Cambodia.

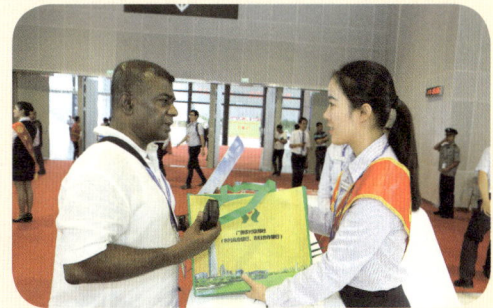

Guangxi Rural Credit Union has actively served the China-ASEAN Exposition, providing multilingual services such as English, Cantonese, Hakka and so on; the Union has set up a bridge between the Credit Union and domestic and foreign businessmen.

China Development Bank has vigorously supported the construction of "Belt and Road Initiative" in the areas of infrastructure, energy resources, new energy, etc, with focuses on supporting the Siem Reap Airport in Cambodia, HPC nuclear power in the United Kingdom, wind power projects in Jarmupir, Pakistan, and the San Gawang, and No. 3 Hydropower Station in Peru, as demonstration of best practices.

Industrial and Commercial Bank of China, as the lead bank of the syndicate, has provided a USD1.44 billion loan for the Sahiwar coal-fired power station project in Pakistan, which is large-scale high-efficiency clean coal power project in the China-Pakistan Economic Corridor. The estimated annual power generation of about 9 billion kilowatt-hours can effectively alleviate the local electricity shortage situation and promote the improvement of people's livelihood and economic and social development in Pakistan.

Landing of key projects

Bank of China has provided financing support for a series of major projects, such as the coal-fired power plant in the Middle East, the Haxiang Clean Energy Power Station in Dubai, and the West Africa's largest man-made commercial seaport, the Ghana Tema Port Construction Project, and facilitated China's high-speed rail, nuclear power, Ultra-High Voltage (UHV), 4G telecommunications and other advantageous industries to "go abroad".

Industrial Bank has stepped up its financial support to major ports, major railways, maritime logistics and port adjacent industries, and has fully taken its comprehensive advantages in the areas of banking, trust, funds, etc. to provide financial support for the infrastructure construction of the nine provinces, autonomous regions and municipalities in the west covered by the "Belt and Road Initiative".

China Minsheng Bank's "New Railway Integrated Logistics Center Project" successfully landed and helped to accelerate the construction of the "Belt and Road Initiative"

By the end of 2017, China Development Bank had provided special loans to SMEs in more than 32 African countries, with a total promising loan balance of USD4.19 billion and a total issued loan balance of USD1.94 billion. The provided loans have supported the areas of agriculture, forestry, farming, manufacturing, trade and other sectors relevant to people's livelihood, created 87 000 jobs which indirectly benefited 470 000 households in the agricultural sector, and created trade revenue of USD2.03 billion.

Guangxi Beibu Gulf Bank has taken advantages of the specialties of people and small and micro enterprises on the border, promoted the innovation of micro-loan products and the construction of data-based, scenario-based and model-based business systems for micro-finance. The bank has vigorously supported the funding of financial services for small and medium-sized scientific and technological enterprises along the border with the balance of RMB71.46 million in 2017; the "cross-border electronic settlement platform" was launched, which has provided convenient services for enterprises and residents along the border including online settlement and sale of foreign exchange, cross-border RMB collection, anti-money laundering, declaration international receipts and payments. The bank has introduced a business of buy-outs of accounts receivable under short-term export credit insurance. With the strengthened cooperation with Chinese export credit insurance companies, the bank has provided credit support to small/micro export enterprises which qualifies for the list of the premium-free by China Export & Credit Insurance Coorperation, and completed export credit insurance financing of USD320 000 in 2017.

Livelihood improvement

Guangxi Rural Credit Union has actively promoted cooperation with Vietnamese commercial banks and put forth efforts to support the construction of international border trade ports. By the end of 2017, three Vietnamese commercial banks had signed border trade settlement business cooperation agreements, and achieved business volume of RMB1.24 billion. The Union has vigorously supported the construction of border trade ports. In 2017, it has issued RMB351 million for port construction loans, supported the construction of six ports, such as the ports of Ningming, Jingxi, Pingxiang, Huai, Dongxing and Longzhou, and supported agricultural enterprises at the ports in carrying out transnational businesses. In 2017, the Union has supported 66 "Belt and Road" enterprises with loans of RMB6.1 billion, 25 more enterprises, and RMB3.8 billion more than the same period last year. Responding positively to the policy spirit of the autonomous region government on "maintaining border stability and promoting the harmonious and sustainable development of border trade," the bank innovated and developed loan products, and increased the credit supply to facilitate border people's production and life, and continuously improved the quality of border financial services. As of the end of 2017, Longzhou, Daxin and other 8 border county-level rural cooperative institutions had provided loans of RMB2.7 billion to 35 534 households in border areas.

Agricultural Bank of China and the Government of Congo (Brazzaville) have jointly formed Sino-Congolese Bank for Africa and signed "the Agreement on deepening Financial Strategic Cooperation and Cross-border RMB Financial Services". The Sino-Congolese Bank for Africa has committed to expanding the RMB trade settlement and exchange business, making efforts to realize the application and promotion of the renminbi in the Central African region.

Bank of China has continued to consolidate its status as the main channel for cross-border circulation of the renminbi, to serve cross-border trade and investment of enterprises, to lead the innovation of international products and services of the renminbi, and to promote the development of the international monetary function of the renminbi. The bank has steadily promoted the renminbi's international status. In 2017, 13 new emerging market currencies, including Nassai, Sri Lankan rupee and Bengal Taka, were added, with 61 non-RMB currencies quoted in foreign exchange. Of the 23 clearing banks designated by The People's Bank of China, 11 are branches of Banks of China, with RMB349.68 trillion for cross-border RMB settlement and RMB3.83 trillion for settlement; Bank of China, as lead underwriter, has assisted 12 of overseas sovereign and sovereign-equivalent organizations, foreign non-financial enterprises, foreign financial institutions and other issuers to issue panda bonds in the interbank market, with a total size of RMB37 billion.

Shanghai Pudong Development Bank has actively prompted RMB internationalization. In response to the call for introducing inward capital investment, under the full range of macro-prudential policy support, the bank introduced the overseas direct loan business version 2.0 to facilitate enterprises to introduce low-cost funds from abroad with reduced financial costs; to meet the demand for cross-border management of RMB, combined with the policy reform and innovation of Shanghai Free Trade Zone, the bank has developed a full-function cross-border two-way RMB fund pool service, which has injected new vitality into the development of the real economy and the internationalization of the renminbi, cooperated with the introduction of CIPS system to enhance the recognition and participation of CIPS system in the international market.

(4) Promoting the Innovation-driven Development

Banking financial institutions have always adhered to problem-oriented focus on the difficulties and weak links of the development of manufacturing and make more efforts to financially support the scientific and technological innovation and the upgrading of the industry. The specialization and refinement of financial services have been improved via the construction of the advanced financing units of manufacturing as well as the specialized institutions for science and technology finance. Banking financial institutions have also innovated and developed the credit management systems and financial product systems that conform to the characteristics of the manufacturing industry so as to actively meet the capital needs of the innovative manufacturing enterprises, maintained a tight focus on the key areas and key tasks of "Made in China 2025", improved the financial services for the manufacturing industry, and promoted the restructuring, transformation and upgrading of the manufacturing industry, as well as the enhancement of quality and efficiency.

▶ Banks in Action

China Development Bank has served "Made in China 2025" strategy actively, participated in the planning of key industries like the national strategic emerging industries, and opened up a new phase of strategic emerging industries, implemented the strategy of the development of the civil-military integration, promoted the transformation and upgrading of the manufacturing industry, and focused on supporting key areas such as integrated circuits, new energy vehicles, and new materials. In 2017, loans to strategic emerging industries totaled RMB344.3 billion, with a year-on-year rise of 45.2 %.

Large commercial banks have closely followed the road map of the national scientific and technological innovation and the layout of the industry chain, fully explored and supported the new model of strategic emerging industries, actively developed and improved the diversified financial organization system that facilitates the building of a manufacturing power. By the end of 2017, Agricultural Bank of China had added RMB45.7 billion in loans to strategic emerging industries in 2017, while Bank of China had granted the balance of credit of RMB493.1 billion to strategic emerging industries.

Shanghai Pudong Development Bank has set up a "1 + 6" science and technology financial center at headquarter level; applying intensive management scheme, headquarter took the lead to coordinate and promote the construction of the exclusive system of science, technology and finance of the whole bank. The bank has created a comprehensive, professional, one-stop digital platform, and constantly upgraded the sci-tech financial service program to serve the development of scientific and technological innovation enterprises. Ping An Bank has founded a development fund for science and technology city industry with RMB25.01 billion, strongly supporting sci-tech production projects. China Zheshang Bank and the Expert Committee on Intelligent Manufacturing of Zhejiang Province have cooperated in depth to innovate a professional service program of "financing assets, facilities, and services" for the intelligent manufacturing. By resorting to various approaches including buyer's credit, equipment outsourcing, financial leasing and so on, the institutions have achieved a rapid development of maritime high-end equipment manufacturing industry, advanced port manufacturing industry, and the optimization and upgrading of maritime industry system.

City Commercial Banks such as Bank of Beijing and Bank of Chongqing actively provided credit resources to high-end manufacturing, Internet of things, biopharmaceutical and other fields, and a basket of financial services such as M & A loans and structural financing. Great efforts have been put in supporting important innovative development projects, major sci-tech specialized projects, and leading enterprises in science and technology so that the strategy of innovation-driven development can be fully implemented.

Innovative Models for Inclusive Finance

(1) Building Inclusive Financial Systems

(2) Facilitating Targeted Poverty Alleviation

(3) Upgrading Financial Services for Agriculture, Rural Areas and Farmers

(4) Supporting the Growth of Small and Micro Enterprises

It is necessary to develop inclusive finance in order to build a well-off society in an all-round way in our country. Banking financial institutions will combine inclusive finance with their own transformation and development, actively explore commercial sustainability, build a system of financial products and services, strengthen financial infrastructure, and raise the level of scientific and technological application, build an online platform of financial service, enhance the financial availability of weak areas, improve the ecological environment of inclusive finance, and constantly improve the people's sense of gain of financial services.

(1) Building Inclusive Financial Systems

Banking financial institutions have continuously prompted the construction of the division of inclusive finance, popularized the financial network of inclusive finance to rural areas, expanded the network of inclusive financial services, established and improved the mechanism of inclusive financial services system, and enhanced the capacity of inclusive financial services. The inclusive finance system helped guide financial resources to key areas and weak links, achieve a wide coverage and multi-level institutional supply system, liberalize financial resources, and provide end-to-end financial services.

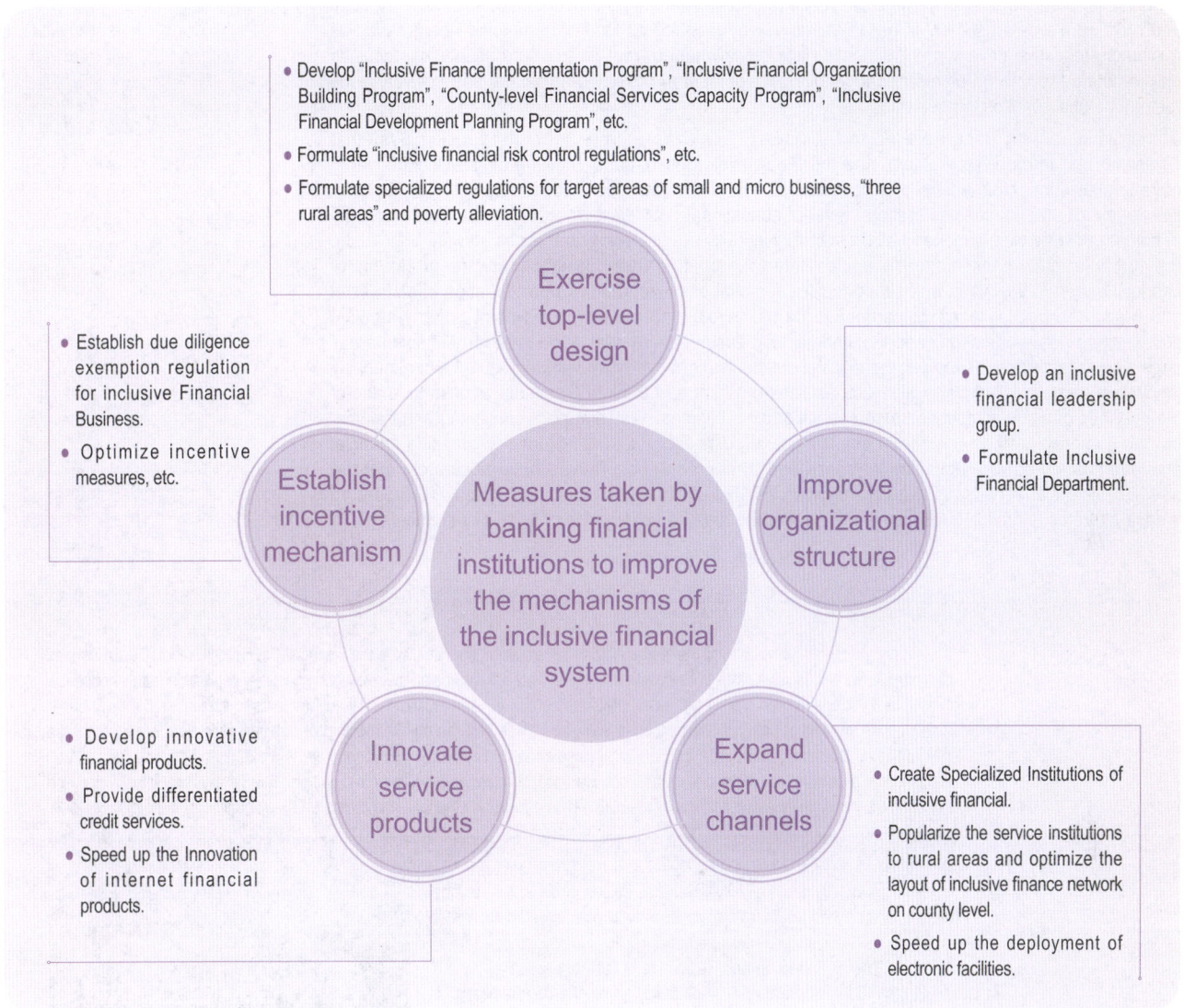

- Develop "Inclusive Finance Implementation Program", "Inclusive Financial Organization Building Program", "County-level Financial Services Capacity Program", "Inclusive Financial Development Planning Program", etc.
- Formulate "inclusive financial risk control regulations", etc.
- Formulate specialized regulations for target areas of small and micro business, "three rural areas" and poverty alleviation.

- Establish due diligence exemption regulation for inclusive Financial Business.
- Optimize incentive measures, etc.

- Develop an inclusive financial leadership group.
- Formulate Inclusive Financial Department.

Exercise top-level design

Establish incentive mechanism

Measures taken by banking financial institutions to improve the mechanisms of the inclusive financial system

Improve organizational structure

Innovate service products

Expand service channels

- Develop innovative financial products.
- Provide differentiated credit services.
- Speed up the Innovation of internet financial products.

- Create Specialized Institutions of inclusive financial.
- Popularize the service institutions to rural areas and optimize the layout of inclusive finance network on county level.
- Speed up the deployment of electronic facilities.

▶ Banks in Action

Agricultural Bank of China has set up the "three rural issues" financial / inclusive financial development committee at the level of the board of directors of the head office, a management committee of the "three rural issues" inclusive financial business division at the level of senior managers, and eight support centers in middle and backdesks. Full coverage of inclusive financial services institutions has been achieved in the first batch of 16 "made in China" pilot demonstration cities (clusters).

Postal Savings Bank of China has extended the reform of the Financial Division of "three Rural issues" throughout the country, established a management mechanism of four levels of structure and three tiers, and an operating mechanism of "seven independent and two tilted", so as to realize the coordination between wholesale and retail. The scope of service has now covered all kinds of agricultural management subjects, and with the embedded function of credit examination and approval, the business efficiency has been improved.

(2) Facilitating Targeted Poverty Alleviation

As an important force in poverty alleviation, banking financial institutions have fully brought into play the diversified advantages and complementary effects of development, policy, commercial and cooperative finance, aiming at the main people and primary tasks to overcome poverty. The organizations have carried out in-depth poverty alleviation cooperation between the east and the west, focused on the "three regions, three states" and other deep poverty-stricken areas, and innovated the modes of credit services and financing for poverty alleviation according to local conditions. Moreover, strong financial supports have been provided to reach the goal of winning the battle against poverty by 2020 and building a well-off society in an all-round way by meeting all kinds of financing needs, such as relocation, industrial development, schooling and employment of registered poor households, focusing on promoting the driving force for endogenous development in poverty eradication, and cultivating the "hematopoietic" function in poor areas.

China Development Bank adhered to the poverty alleviation strategy of "Introducing Systems, Financing and Introducing Wisdom" and the "Four levels destinations" thinking of "provincial level of poverty alleviation, county level of infrastructure construction, villages (households) level of business development, and households (people) level of educational subsidies". In 2017, "three major actions" to combat poverty was launched which effectively increased support for poor areas and the population. Policy banks have conscientiously implemented the guiding ideology and target requirements of financial poverty alleviation, and supported the removal of poverty hat of poor counties in state-level and registered poor villages. In particular, the old revolutionary areas, fixed-point poverty-stricken counties and policy-oriented financial experimental areas of poverty alleviation in poverty-stricken areas should be regarded as the top priority, and the mechanism of poverty alleviation should be continuously innovated. Large commercial banks such as Bank of China and Bank of Communications made use of the methods of credit investment, resource integration, business matchmaking, consulting and training, etc., to explore an efficient mode of financially and sustainably alleviating poverty. Banking financial institutions such as rural commercial banks and rural credit cooperatives have accurately met the needs of financial services in deep poverty-stricken areas of the province, and effectively supported infrastructure construction in extremely poor townships and the governance of human settlements.

By the end of 2017[1]

RMB **249.69** billion micro credit loan issued to alleviate poverty

6.07 million registered poor households supported

the coverage of basic financial services in poverty-stricken counties' administrative villages had reached

95.83%
increased by **2.93** percentage points from the beginning of the year

▶ Banks in Action

China Development Bank has played the leading role of development finance, taken the Financial Poverty Alleviation Department as the "group army" in a decisive battle to overcome poverty, and steadily promoted the relocation of poverty population from inhospitable areas. The bank has worked closely with relevant ministries and departments and local governments to implement the spirit of the State Council meeting of promoting relocation in some provinces and the on-site meeting of national relocation, so as to ensure sufficient funds for the relocation task; the bank paid close attention to poverty alleviation in areas with extreme poverty, tracked and promoted key projects in key regions such as Tibet, Guizhou, Yunnan, and the "three regions and three prefectures", innovated and supported the poverty alleviation projects of the state reserve forest in Guangxi, and promoted the relocation of the registered poor population from forest regions. In 2017, an addition of RMB56 billion loans have been issued to help the poor, with a cumulative commitment of RMB448.3 billion, benefiting 9.11 million registered poor people.

Agricultural Development Bank of China has strictly followed the national and provincial "13th Five-Year Plan" for poverty alleviation and relocation to formulate the "Special Loan Measures of Agricultural Development Bank of China for Poverty Reduction and Relocation in Different Areas (revised in 2017)," and further improved the credit policy for aid-the-poor relocation in the area to ensure that loans are legal and compliant; preferential policies for poverty alleviation has been increased to actively support poverty alleviation and relocation in extreme poverty-stricken areas. With organizational, geographical and policy advantages, the bank has provided new ways to support the development of innovative credit for the subsequent industrial development of poverty alleviation and relocation in different areas. By the end of 2017, the balance of loans for poverty alleviation and relocation in different areas had amounted to RMB253.86 billion, benefiting 7.68 million relocated people, 5.24 million of whom were registered poor people.

Guangxi Beibu Gulf Bank has responded positively to the "Tianyang County 13th Five-Year Plan for Poverty Alleviation and Relocation", awarded RMB50 million credit to make up for the funding gap of the resettlement project, and helped 45 180 poor people of 13 183 households in Tianyang County relocate in an all-round way.

Chongqing Rural Commercial Bank has included anti-poverty micro-credit policy to formulate exclusive credit products of "poverty assistance loans", and focused on supporting the households from mountainous areas to relocate.

Relocation from Inhospitable Areas

China Development Bank supported the relocation project in Wugang City

Agricultural Development Bank of China supported poverty alleviation and relocation project in Tongjiang County, Sichuan Province

[1] Data source: China Banking and Insurance Regulatory Commission.

Industrial and Commercial Bank of China has made full use of Internet financial means to build a sale platform for high-quality agricultural products, effectively promoted e-commerce poverty alleviation in view of the difficulties in sale of agricultural products in poor areas and the fact that good products are "kept in boudoir unrecognized." China Construction Bank has built an e-commerce platform named "Shanrong e-commerce" to help the poor. In 2017, the volume of business transactions made by the platform for poverty alleviation has exceeded RMB5.1 billion, with a cumulative total of more than 1 900 merchants, covering more than 500 poor counties.

China Everbright Bank has popularized the e-commerce model of targeted poverty alleviation through a platform called "Yunnan·Gou Jing Cai" and successfully explored a new path to e-commerce poverty alleviation. By the end of 2017, more than 20 000 items of goods had been sold on the platform, with a sales volume of nearly RMB6 million.

E-commerce platform of China Everbright Bank helped the sale of NujiangChangmao rice

Guangxi Rural Credit Union has actively carried out an e-commerce poverty alleviation campaign with the advantages of the financial service network throughout the region and nationwide, provided a network marketing platform for agricultural products to help poor farmers sell LingshanMaogu orange, litchi, Hezhou San Hua plums, Baise mango, Rong County Shatian pomelo and other agricultural products to 25 provinces, helped farmers to increase production and income.

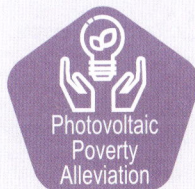

Poverty Alleviation with e-commerce

Agricultural Bank of China has continued to enrich the characteristics of poverty alleviation products, and actively promoted photovoltaic poverty alleviation model based on the good natural foundation of photovoltaic power generation in poor areas. By the end of 2017, the balance of photovoltaic loans for poverty alleviation had reached RMB2.5 billion, supported 235 projects and leaded to an increase in the income of 156 000 poor people, among whom there were 17 000 poor households who directly enjoyed the installing of photovoltaic power generation system.

Postal Savings Bank of China has developed photovoltaic anti-poverty micro-credit products, and gradually piloted the photovoltaic anti-poverty small loans in Shanxi, Anhui, Hebei and other 26 provinces and cities. The loans have effectively solved the problem of farmers' lacking funds to install power generation equipments. By the end of 2017, a total of 6 300 photovoltaic poverty alleviation small loans had been issued, amounted to more than RMB358 million.

Bank of Jiangsu and other city commercial banks have visited key poverty alleviation offices of Jiangsu Province, Development and Reform Commissions and enterprises that implemented the photovoltaic poverty alleviation projects, and completed in-depth field research. Combining the existing photovoltaic loans and photovoltaic industry funds and other products, and the banks have formulated corresponding financing projects and increased the loans for targeted poverty alleviation according to different types of programs such as village-level power stations and state-level power stations.

Liaoning Rural Credit Cooperatives has provided a loan of RMB25 million to support the development of photovoltaic industry in Jianchang County. The photovoltaic industry has effectively taken the local advantages of longer day lighting period, and abundant solar energy resources, lifting 11 000 people out of poverty.

Photovoltaic Poverty Alleviation

The joint-stock banks such as China CITIC Bank and China Zheshang Bank have actively promoted products such as "residential accommodation loan" in accordance with local resource condition in different places, and actively supported the development of poverty alleviation tourism in poor areas.

Working with professional organizations such as the Tourism Commission, Bank of Beijing has provided credit loans for ethnicity related tourism businesses to help poor rural areas with abundant tourism resources to get rid of poverty.

Zhejiang Chouzhou Commercial Bank has carried out poverty alleviation projects based on the characteristics of the local human environment, explored effective targeted poverty alleviation approaches by supporting residential arts and crafts and other cultural tourism industry. By the end of 2017, a total of RMB120 million of loans had been issued to support the development of root carving craft in Quzhou, helping the construction of China's root carving cultural industrial park and promoting the masses to get rid of poverty and become rich.

Financial institutions such as Zhejiang Rural Credit Cooperatives and Inner Mongolia Rural Credit Cooperatives have actively utilized rural tourism resources and innovated the credit support mode of tourism poverty alleviation. The Cooperatives have further integrated the development of primary, secondary, and tertiary industries, such as "agritainment" in rural areas so that poor households in poverty can have better access to wealth and jobs.

Poverty Alleviation with Tourism

(3) Upgrading Financial Services for Agriculture, Rural Areas and Farmers

The banking financial institutions have conscientiously implemented the Party Central Committee's strategy for rural revitalization, adhered to the main line of structural reform on the supply side of agriculture, focused on solving the problem of uneven development, and actively promoted the return of various types of agri-banking institutions to their original functions. In the fields of national food security, agricultural and rural infrastructure construction, agricultural and rural modernization, and so on, the institutions have innovated and explored the service mode suitable for the new type of agricultural operators, constantly improved the rural financial system, and activated the rural financial market, actively contributed to provide new financial driving force for writing the new chapter of the "Three Rural development" of China.

By the end of 2017[①]

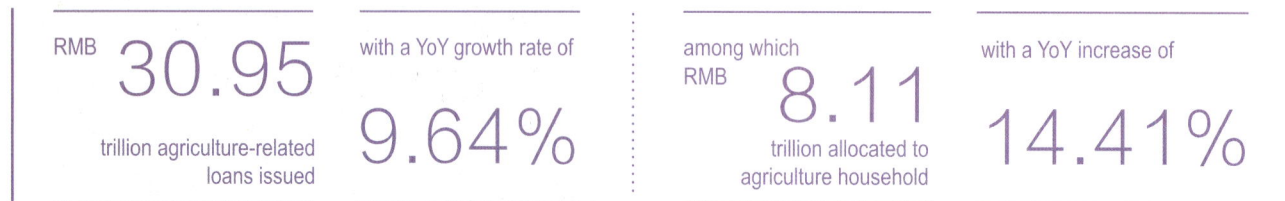

| RMB **30.95** trillion agriculture-related loans issued | with a YoY growth rate of **9.64%** | among which RMB **8.11** trillion allocated to agriculture household | with a YoY increase of **14.41%** |

▶ Banks in Action

Agricultural Development Bank of China has defined the responsibility of the agricultural policy-based banks, promulgated the guidance opinion of Agricultural Development Bank of China on the strategy of serving the rural areas, and regarded the strategy of serving the rural revitalization as the core responsibility and central task of the new era. The bank has increased the long-term credit investment in rural revitalization, supported agricultural modernization and green development, gave prominence to ensuring national food security, promoted green agriculture, improved farmers' production and living conditions, and gave full play to the guiding and supplementary role of policy-based finance. Great efforts have been made to achieve goals that the rural revitalization should make great progress by 2020 and institutional framework and policy system should be basically formed. By the end of 2017, the balance of medium-term and long-term loans for the construction of agricultural and rural infrastructure had reached RMB2.53 trillion, and RMB98.8 billion of various agricultural modernization loans were issued throughout the year, supported the establishment of 21.97 million mu of high-standard farmland.

Large commercial banks, such as Agricultural Bank of China, have always adhered to serving the "three rural issues". With a strong commitment to promote development in country areas, the large commercial banks have conformed to the new changes, new characteristics and new trends of the agricultural and rural economy, and vigorously implemented the strategy of rural revitalization. Focusing on serving "Big Three Rural Issues", "New Three Rural Issues" and "Distinctive Three Rural Issues", the large commercial banks have constantly upgraded the level of financial services for agriculture, rural areas and farmers, promoted stronger agriculture, more beautiful rural areas, richer farmers, and started a new journey in the financial cause of agriculture, rural areas and farmers.

Postal Savings Bank of China has put the development of agricultural economy and the increase of farmers' income in a prominent position. In 2017, the bank has speeded up the improvement of the operational mechanism of the financial department of "Three Rural Issues", popularized and completed the reform of the financial department of "Three Rural Issues" in 27 branches throughout the country, and optimized the management mechanism for serving the "three rural issues". Following the development thinking of "one county, one industry, one line of goods and one product", the bank has innovated investment and financing mode, served 378 national key agricultural leading enterprises in agricultural industrialization, with a coverage rate of 30.43%, and vigorously enhanced financial support to the core enterprises of the agricultural industrial chain and upstream and downstream customers. By the end of 2017, the balance of agriculture-related loans had reached RMB1.05 trillion, accounted for 30.881% of the bank's total loan balance, the balance of small loans had reached RMB156.43 billion, and the balance of loans for new agricultural operators increased by RMB13.02 billion, with a 42.97% rise compared to the end of last year.

Joint-stock banks such as China Guangfa Bank and PingAn Bank have grasped the new trend of the development of national agricultural industrialization, used the advantages of comprehensive finance and financial science and technology to support the improvement of agricultural production technology, the prevention and control of agricultural non-point source pollution, and the industrial chain customers of leading enterprises, promoted the upstream and downstream agricultural production development, and further highlighted the green, ecological, safe and inclusive nature of "Three Rural Issues".

Harbin Bank has enriched the credit product system of agriculture, and has met the financing needs of agriculture, rural areas and farmers in all directions. Harbin Bank has also provided rural land contractual management rights and agricultural facilities mortgage loan services throughout the province, effectively invigorated rural stock assets, improved the utilization efficiency of rural property rights resources, innovated the introduction of farmers' specialized cooperative loans and family farm loans, etc. A diversified "new-type agricultural management main body" product system, which has covered large scale breeding households, family farms, farmers' specialized cooperatives and agriculture-related leading enterprises have established to create and promote the e loan featuring "Internet + benefiting agriculture" and to help the development of new rural finance.

Based on the local advantages, Bank of Qingdao focused on developing new agriculture, marine fishery and other characteristic industries, made full use of the geographical location advantages of marine fisheries, deeply investigated the patterns of development of local marine fisheries, and continuously innovated the application of products. The bank has supported the financing needs of large and medium-sized aquaculture and fishing enterprises within the jurisdiction and made every effort to promote the development of modern agriculture. By the end of 2017, the balance of marine fishery loans to the public had reached RMB387.7 million.

① Data source:China Banking and Insurance Regulatory Commission.

Tianjin Rural Commercial Bank has continued to promote the construction of financial service stations and financial convenience service points, so that farmers can enjoy basic financial services such as small cash deposits and withdrawals without leaving their home in a better financial payment environment in rural areas. By the end of 2017, a total of 1 085 financial service stations had been set up in the jurisdiction, and 1 423 financial services had been accessible to the people, basically realizing the coverage of financial services in villages with more than a thousand people.

Guangzhou Rural Commercial Bank, headquartered in Southern Guangdong, has adhered to the management aim of serving agriculture, rural areas and farmers and formed a diversified and extensive financial service channel composed of rural financial service stations, agricultural withdrawal points, mobile banks, etc., trying to clear off the difficulties in the conduction of plans for serving "three rural issues".

Xiamen Rural Commercial Bank has actively expanded financial service channels to deal with the "three rural issues", promoted the implementation of "3 in 1" working mode of rural household filing, accurate filing, and agricultural e-loan. By the end of 2017, there had been 4 159 contracts for non-paper and no-guarantee "agricultural e-loans", amounting to RMB157 million.

Jiangxi Rural Credit Union has explored and created new credit models such as "Agricultural and Commercial Bank + leading Enterprises + Farmers" and "Agricultural and Commercial Bank + Farmers' Professional Cooperatives + Professional Farmers", combining core enterprises with high-quality farmers. In 2017, the Credit Union has started business with 1 001 leading enterprises, 9 983 farmers' professional cooperatives, 5 493 family farms, 22 410 professional large households, and 529 other new types of business operators, granting RMB20.78 billion of credit, encouraged more than 162,532 households to start a business.

Inner Mongolia Rural Credit Cooperatives has adhered to the market orientation of serving the urban and rural communities and "three agriculture and three pastoralism," and given priority to ensuring the traditional agricultural and animal husbandry production fund needs, supporting grain production, the development of modern animal husbandry, the industrialization of agriculture and animal husbandry, and the innovation of agricultural and animal husbandry production and management methods, and vigorously promoted the development of new types of agricultural and animal husbandry business entities, such as family farming and pastures, large farmers, and professional cooperatives. By the end of 2017, the balance of agricultural and pastoral loans for rural credit cooperatives in the whole region had reached RMB184.38 billion.

Sichuan Rural Credit Union has actively implemented the mode of credit management and promotion of farmers' credit, which features "once approved, loan on demand, balance control, turnover intention and dynamic adjustment", and has established economic archives for 13.31 million households throughout the province. In 2017, RMB270.8 billion had been granted to 1.46 million farmers to support the development of green farming and aquaculture.

Gansu Rural Credit Union has formulated the "guidance opinions on the Marketing of Agricultural loans in 2017" and "the Circular on doing a good Job in preparing for farming and Financial Services in Spring ploughing", and has actively adjusted the credit structure. The Credit Union has specifically prepared financial resources for grain production and characteristic industries, and precisely met the new needs of high quality, high efficiency and green agriculture to promote the modernization of agriculture and the urbanization of rural areas.

HSBC Rural Bank has paid great attention to and participated in the rural financial reform of China. The bank has always taken the promotion of local economic development of "three rural issues" as its own responsibility, and devoted itself to extending the international financial services to the forefront of the rural market step by step. By the end of 2017, loans involving farmers and small and micro enterprises had totaled RMB1.11 billion, accounting for 92% of all loans.

Postal Savings Bank of China genuinely served farmers

China Development Bank supported industrialization project of Modern Agricultural Plant Factory of Chinese Medicine

Guangxi Rural Credit Union introduced new agricultural loans to meet the financial needs of farmers in the process of production and operation

(4) Supporting the Growth of Small and Micro Enterprises

Banking financial institutions have followed the principle of "implementing policies according to the enterprises' conditions and providing differentiated services", effectively used the Internet, big data, cloud computing, artificial intelligence and other emerging financial technologies, continued to innovate personalized services and micro-credit products, built a cooperation platform, contributed funds and wisdom, promoted the construction of franchises, improved the quality of service, expanded the coverage of services, solved the financing difficulties of small and micro enterprises, finance expensive problems, and effectively promoted the healthy development of small and micro enterprises.

By the end of 2017[1]

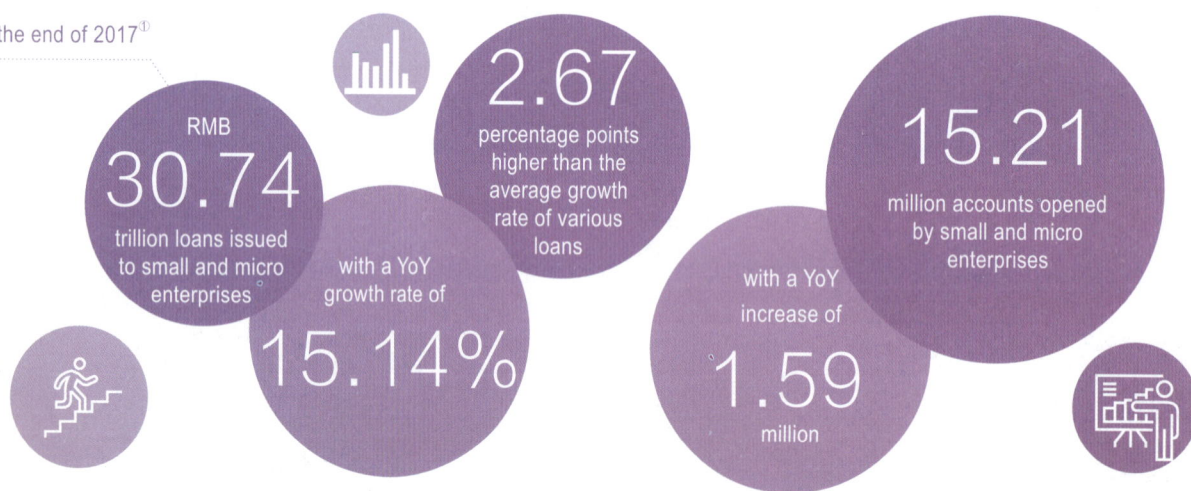

RMB **30.74** trillion loans issued to small and micro enterprises

with a YoY growth rate of **15.14%**

2.67 percentage points higher than the average growth rate of various loans

with a YoY increase of **1.59** million

15.21 million accounts opened by small and micro enterprises

Agricultural Development Bank of China has actively carried out pilot work in Zhejiang and Jiangxi in the business of "supporting agriculture and transferring loans". Large commercial banks, such as Industrial and Commercial Bank of China and Bank of China, have promoted the construction of inclusive finance outlets to enhance the credit service capacity of grass-roots branches and continuously improve the product service system for small and medium-sized enterprises. Join-stock banks such as China CITIC Bank, China Everbright Bank and China Zheshang Bank tilted the distribution of credit resources, built small and micro "credit factories", and innovated and renewed loan products; Bank of Beijing and other city commercial banks have set up small and micro batch cooperation platforms, widely carried out cooperation between banks and enterprises as well as banks and Tax Bureau, strengthened the construction of franchises, and taken products as the starting point to strengthen small and micro services.

According to the financing needs of the market and small and micro enterprises, banking financial institutions have continuously innovated the financial products for small and micro enterprises, explored and brought forth new ideas in practice, and formed a rich and colorful system of products and services. Many new financial applications have been therefore created, such as the "Cai Fu Dai" from Industrial and Commercial Bank of China, the funding application from Bank of China, the "Small-micro Enterprise Online Financing System from China Everbright Bank of China, "E-commerce Loan" APP for small and micro enterprises from Huaxia Bank , "Three Pertinent Credit Products" from Industrial Bank, the "People's livelihood Project of Small and Medium-sized Enterprises" from China Minsheng Bank, "Easy Loan" from China Zheshang Bank, "Hao Qi Dai" from Bank of Chongqing, and so on. The various product systems have constructed a good ecological finance system, and enhanced the financial service efficiency for small and micro enterprises with flexibility, fastness and efficiency.

[1] Data source:China Banking and Insurance Regulatory Commission.

Postal Savings Bank of China has set up a win-win cooperation platform and successfully signed strategic cooperation agreements with Ministry of Industry and Information Technology of the People's Republic of China and Shanghai Stock Exchange. The bank has vigorously promoted various cooperation projects with sectors such as science and technology, and industry and commerce, and fully utilized the advantages as the information sharing platform between "the bank and the government, the bank and the association, the bank and enterprises, the bank and guarantee agencies," shared risks and strived to improve the financing environment for small and medium-sized enterprises. In 2017, a total of RMB760.75 billion was granted to small and micro enterprises.

China Zheshang Bank has established a special small and micro financial product research and development team which worked around the guarantee mode, efficiency, quota, deadline and other issues concerned by small and micro business owners, and formed a system containing a wide range of characteristic products. The bank has introduced new loans of "San Ban Dai" for emerging markets, "Chuangying Dai" to combine the bank's investment and loan services; the bank has also launched loans of "Wen Chuang Dai", "Kechuang Loan" to support cultural and technological development; launched "Xin Yong Tong" with flexible credit limit, a loan of "Min Su Dai" to help homestay business; introduced settlement products such as "Account Link" and "Small-micro Settlement Card"; strongly promoted products with innovative repayment methods, such as "Three-year Loan", "Easy Loan", "Maturity Loan" and "Continuous Loan".

Taking into account various cost factors including capital, risk and operation, Bank of Jiangsu has developed pricing models and systems for small and micro enterprises , implemented refined pricing and effectively controlled the financing cost; at the same time, the bank has made great efforts to actively give reduction and exemption from certain charges under control of an automatic system. In 2017, the initiative fee reduction had amounted to nearly RMB30 million.

Mr. Yang, an engineer with the support of small business loan from China Zheshang Bank, transferred in an enterpreneur of smart home business

Jiangxi Bank has actively responded to the requirements of "Notice of the China Banking Regulatory Commission on Further Implementing the Regulatory Policies on Financial Services for Micro and Small Enterprises" issued preferential policies, created new loan services to provide cash flow for the approved enterprises. The approved enterprises can renew the loan without repaying with a new loan, which has effectively lowered the cost and simplified the approving process. By the end of 2017, the balance of renewed loan had amounted to 13.25 billion with over 1 634 transactions.

Bank of Hangzhou has established a new channel to apply for loans. The bank has provided many electronic application channels through WeChat, mobilebanking APP, official website and so on for the "micro-credit card" business, and application function through QR code for the "micro-credit card" and "cloud mortgage"business. Customers can initiate applications through the aforementioned electronic channels or the sharing links from the account managers. In addition, customers can also generate their exclusive QR code for preservation which enhances financial services in all aspects.

As a Hong Kong based banking company, Hang Seng Bank (China) has been focuing on its business development in the Pearl River Delta region. The bank started to work with an export insurance company since 2009. Together with its parent bank in Hong Kong and its Macao branch, they have jointly signed the export credit insurance bank policy across Hong Kong, Macao and mainland China. With the bank policy, small and medium-sized export enterprises can directly apply for insurance, submit declaration form and make a claim through the bank, thus greatly reducing the management costs of the enterprises. Meanwhile, the enterprises can also enjoy the preferential pricing of bank policy and reduce the premium burden. To a certain extent, the bank policy can solve the problem of asymmetry between cost and benefit in the financing of small and medium-sized enterprises.

China Construction Bank visited small business clients to understand their production and operation, and customized a comprehensive financial service plan

Huaxia Bank visited small business clients

Understanding the Needs and Optimizing Customer Service

(1) Leading the Improvement of Quality and Efficiency of Services

(2) Expanding Service Channels

(3) Safeguarding the Rights and Interests of Consumers

With the core value of "customer orientation", the banking financial institutions have made strategic plans for cultural cultivation, and have actively played a leading role in financial science and technology, made full use of Internet technology and big data analysis, and provided customers with more comprehensive and convenient services. On one hand, the institutions have continued to adjust and optimize the traditional network, integrate and upgrade the existing products and services, and timely promote business transformation. On the other hand, the institutions have made more efforts to improve the construction of consumer rights and interests protection system, integrated the protection of consumer rights and interests into all aspects of business operations, and built a more effective mechanism for consumer protection, in order to constantly improve the quality of service and customer experience.

(1) Leading the Improvement of Quality and Efficiency of Services

In 2017, the banking financial institutions have fully utilized the leading role of the service culture. With multiple measures in use and the formation of advanced concepts, the institutions have formed a unique service culture to enhance the understanding of the service concepts, promote the quality and efficiency of service, improve customers' experience, and showcase a better service image.

▶ **Banks in Action**

Improving the Quality and Efficiency of the Service	Digitalization, networking, intelligence and mobility have made modern social and economic activities more flexible, convenient and intelligent. Financial science and technology have become the driving force for the innovation and development of financial services, and have brought new challenges and opportunities to the banking industry. In 2017, China's banking industry, driven by scientific and technological innovation, has kept in pace with the trend of the times, and continued to strengthen the promotion and application of advanced scientific and technological means and management methods in the financial field under the theme of "inclusion, crossover, safety and efficiency". By changing the traditional banking service mode, China's banking industry has improved the efficiency of service, enhanced the technical kinetic energy on the supply side of the service, and put forth the sustainable and balanced development of the banking industry.
Promoting Transformation and Upgrading of Industry Service	In the face of the new environment of "strong supervision" and the ever-changing social needs, China Banking Association has promptly summarized the work of civilized and standardized service, and upgraded and adjusted the service standard system, maintained the advanced, scientific and leading nature of the evaluation system. The banking institutions in accordance with the new standards have all updated the service management system and optimized the service organizational framework. The overall service quality of the industry has thus been comprehensively upgraded.
Cultivating service model	In order to continue to promote the construction of civilized and standardized service brand system in the industry, to continuously deepen the leading role of high-quality service outlets, and to continuously improve the overall service level and quality of the industry, China Banking Association has organized the 2017 China Banking civilized and standardized service evaluation activities namely "100 Best Units" and "star outlets", displaying the overall image of the industry service. The assessment has gone through a series of deliberations including the self-recommendation, the upgrading through the inspection from banking system, the examination of the local associations and regulatory authorities, the qualification examination of China Banking Association, the on-site inspection and expert consultation, volunteer experience feedback, and final review. A large number of excellent business outlets have emerged. With the modern and intelligent service facilities and high level service quality, the outlets that won the title of "100 Best Units" have set up the image as the industry service benchmark and displayed the beauty of the industry.
Improving Customer Satisfaction	China's banking industry have made persistent efforts to innovate products and services, enrich service channels, improve service processes, pay attention to detail management, and focus on consumer demand. The efforts have yielded satisfactory results as the overall service capacity of the industry has ever been on the rise and so as the customer satisfaction. In 2017, China Consumer Association and China Federation of disabled Persons have conducted a survey on barrier-free facilities in 102 cities of 31 provinces, municipalities and autonomous regions. According to the survey data, the satisfaction on financial services concerning barrier-free facilities has exceeded 75%.

(2) Expanding Service Channels

In 2017, banking financial institutions have accelerated the construction of self-service bank, effectively extended the radius of traditional business outlets services, and improved the county financial services capacity. At the same time, the banking financial institutions have been committed to simplify the process, expand functions, improve intelligence, and provide customers with quality services.

According to incomplete statistics, by the end of 2017[1]

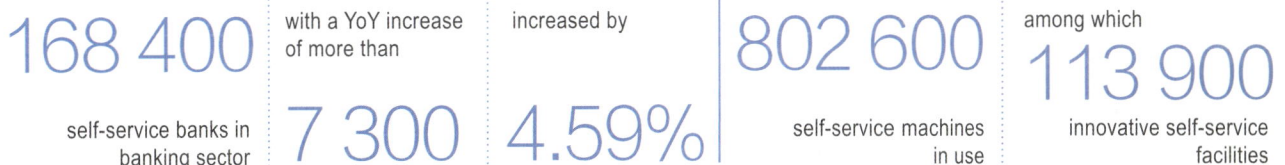

168 400 self-service banks in banking sector	with a YoY increase of more than **7 300**	increased by **4.59%**	**802 600** self-service machines in use	among which **113 900** innovative self-service facilities

① Data source:China Banking Services Report 2017.

40.01
billion transactions handled via
self-service facilities

RMB
66.13
trillion trading volume

with a YoY increase
10.37%

▶ Banks in Action

Optimizing Traditional Service

In 2017, adhering to the customer-oriented principle, the China banking industry has paid close attention to the changes in economic and financial resources and customer financial needs, has comprehensively analyzed the development potential of various business outlets, formulated detailed plans, adjusted and optimized the distribution of branches, improved facilities, refined divisions, and improved the productivity in business outlets. By the end of 2017, the total number of business outlets of banking financial institutions nationwide had reached 228 700. According to incomplete statistics, more than 800 new business outlets had been built and 10 700 business outlets had been renovated during the year.

Deepening Innovation on the e-platforms

In 2017, China's banking industry has proactively complied with the trend of mobile development such as artificial intelligence, big data and block chain, actively applied the latest achievements of financial science and technology, accelerated the intelligent transformation of various channels, and comprehensively opened up customer contact channels. The lowered threshold of financial services has enhanced the experience of customer transactions, and built a competitive advantage of retail finance system. According to incomplete statistics, in 2017, the banking financial institutions had made 260.04 billion off-the-counter transactions, an increase of 46.33% over the same period last year. The off-the-counter transactions had amounted to RMB201.07 billion, an increase of 32.06% over the same period last year. The average rate of off-the-counter business in the industry was 87.58%.

Improving the Effectiveness of Community Banks

In 2017, China's banking industry has adhered to standardization and differentiation development strategy, integrated advantage resources, further standardized the establishment of community banks, small and micro banks, improved the network comprehensive marketing service capacity, and enhanced the development efficiency. By the end of 2017, according to incomplete statistics, China's banking sector had established 7 890 community networks and 2 550 business outlets for micro-enterprises.

Expanding Accessibility

In order to further enhance the level of banking accessibility service in an all-round way and promote the development of the barrier-free environment in China's banking industry to an institutionalized, normalization and standardized level, China Banking Association, in accordance with the "Plan for Furthering the Work Standardization Reforms" (the State council [2015] 13th), the "Plan for the Construction and Development of the Standardization system of the Financial Industry (2016-2020)" jointly released by "One Bank and Three commissions" and Standardization Administration of the People's Public of China, and with the assistance of the China disabled Persons' Federation and others, in 2017, has launched the "Standard for Building a Barrier-free Environment in China's Banking Industry" to standardize and guide financial institutions to better meet the growing financial service needs of clients with disabilities. Efforts have been made to enable clients with disabilities to share the achievements of our country's financial, economic and social development, and high-quality financial services.

Smart Banks Leading Development

In 2017, the China's banking industry has promoted the construction of intelligent banks with intelligent innovation. Through the extensive application of various intelligent technologies and equipment, the banking industry has gradually realized the systematic innovation and reshaping of the bank traditional management mode, management system mechanism, business system and brand culture. The innovations have not only met the customers' needs for diversified services, but also led the development of future transformation.

① Data source:China Banking Services Report 2017.

Intelligent Age of Customer Services

In 2017, China's banking industry has continuously upgraded the service level of the customer service center, strengthened the standardized construction of standards, led the development trend of artificial intelligence, and created the experience of intelligent customer service. According to incomplete statistics, by the end of 2017, 51,200 employees, in total, had worked as customer service staff in banking financial institutions, answered 1.07 billion calls and served 4.21 billion customers over the past year. The average rate of manual call connection in banking customer service center was 91.22%, among which, the rate of credit card customer service line was 93.37%, which has been more than 90% for five consecutive years.

(3) Safeguarding the Rights and Interests of Consumers

In 2017, the banking financial institutions have earnestly implemented the "Law of the people's Republic of China on the Protection of consumers' Rights and interests", the State Council's "Guiding Opinions on Strengthening the Protection of Financial Consumers' Rights and Interests", "Implementation Measures of People's Bank of China On Protecting Financial Consumer Rights and Interests", the original CBRC's "Interim Regulatory Provisions on Audio and Video Recording in the Sales Zones of Banking Institutions", "Guidance on Strengthening the Protection of Banking Consumers' Rights and Interests, and Addressing the Concerns of the Masses", and "Notice on the key points for Consumer Rights and interests Protection in the Banking Industry in 2017", have steadily advanced the construction of the system of consumer rights and interests protection in its own units, and strived to improve the effectiveness of the protection of consumer rights and interests in the banking sector. The banking institutions have taken multiple measures of improving the process, standardized publicity and protected the hardware to meet relevant requirements such as the implementation of the "double records" of sales area and product sales, and standardized product sales behavior, and improved information publicity. Last but not least, the protection of consumers' rights and interests has been integrated into all aspects of banking management.

China's banking industry has continued to organize and promote public education activities in the banking sector. Under the principles of public welfare, timeliness, service and sustainability, the banking institutions have carried out public education actively, regularly, continuously and systematically. By educating the public on financial knowledge and cultivating their financial awareness and ability, potential threats can be prevented and resolved and a harmonious financial consumption environment can be built, which would further prompt the healthy development of the banking industry.

China Banking Association has organized an industry-wide campaign to promote financial literacy for seven consecutive years. In 2017, the event was consisted of three themes, namely "Safe use of payment and settlement account ", "Electronic Intelligent Services Promotion" and "Telecommunication Network Fraud Prevention".

According to incomplete statistics, in 2017[1]

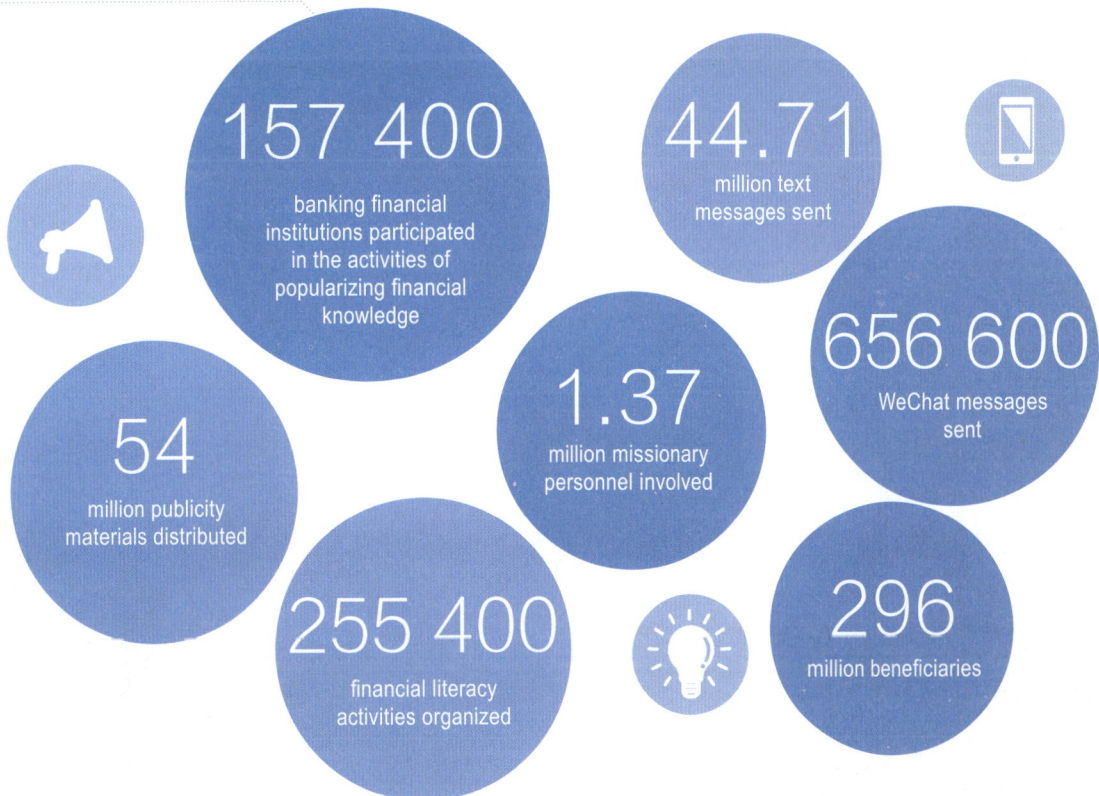

157 400 banking financial institutions participated in the activities of popularizing financial knowledge

44.71 million text messages sent

656 600 WeChat messages sent

54 million publicity materials distributed

1.37 million missionary personnel involved

255 400 financial literacy activities organized

296 million beneficiaries

① Data source:China Banking Services Report 2017.

Protecting Ecology and Promoting Green Development

(1) Developing Green Finance

(2) Implementing Green and Low Carbon Projects

The banking financial institutions have set up the concept that waters and mountains are invaluable assets, supported economic activities of improving the environment, coping with climate change, saving and utilizing resources efficiently, increased investment in green credit, and carry out green office operations, strengthened the management of supply chain, taken actions to ensure environmental protection of green welfare, promoted green and low-carbon economy development, and built a beautiful China.

Agricultural Development Bank of China supported the Zhangjiakou National Reserve Forest Project.

(1) Developing Green Finance

Banking financial institutions have continued to implement the "guidance on Building a Green Financial system", integrated the concept of green credit into strategy, organizational structures, management system and business processes of institutions, and effectively strengthened environmental and social risk management, improved the disclosure of relevant information, actively innovated green financial products and services. Through the issuance of green financial debts, green credit asset transfers and other fund raising methods, the financing needs of low-carbon, recycling, and ecological areas have been met.

By the end of 2017[1]

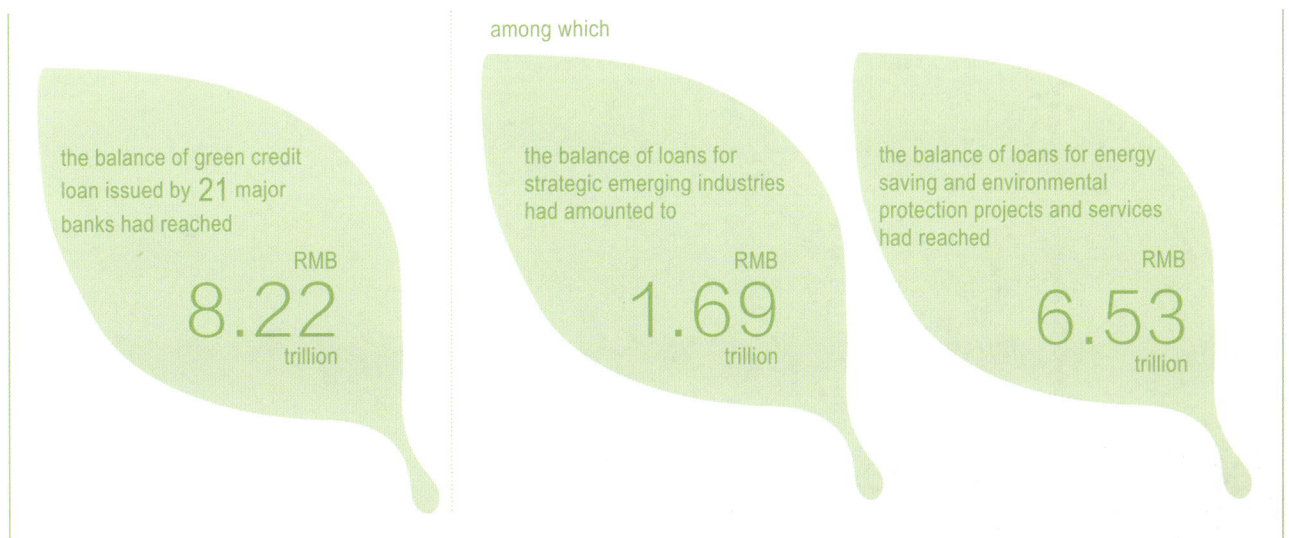

the balance of green credit loan issued by 21 major banks had reached

RMB
8.22
trillion

among which

the balance of loans for strategic emerging industries had amounted to

RMB
1.69
trillion

the balance of loans for energy saving and environmental protection projects and services had reached

RMB
6.53
trillion

[1] Data source:China Banking and Insurance Regulatory Commission.

Improve the System

China Development Bank has improved its institutional construction, standardized projects in the fields of green credit, green financial bond issuance, such as project adjustment, credit review, post-loan management, and so on, and promoted the construction of a mechanism. The bank has participated actively in the research and formulation of green finance policies and financing plans with relevant ministries and local governments, and formulated the "Yangtze River Economic Belt Ecological Protection Investment and financing Plan" for Hubei Province in 2017. The bank has used innovative modes of franchise, PPP and government purchase service, and management of contract energy to support the prevention of air pollution, watershed water environment control and other projects. By the end of 2017, the balance of green credit loans had amounted to RMB 1.64 trillion.

The Export-Import Bank of China has allocated credit resources rationally to promote the development of green, circular and low-carbon economy and to facilitate the promotion of technical innovation projects of enterprises that are high in energy consumption and emission. The bank has continued to increase support for green agriculture development, resource recycling, waste disposal and pollution prevention, renewable energy and clean energy, green transportation, energy conservation and environmental protection services, and industrial energy, water, and environmental protection. By the end of 2017, the balance of green credit had exceeded RMB 100 billion, and the supported projects had reduced the use of standard coal by 17.02 million tons, carbon dioxide by 33 million tons, sulphur dioxide by 111 200 tons, nitrogen oxides by 33 700 tons and water saving by 32.02 million tons. The reduction of pollutants has had significant environmental and social effects.

Industrial Bank has deepened its cooperation with Fujian Green Home Environmental Friendship Center, an environmental non-governmental organization, to incorporate environmental warning information such as the list of pollution Enterprises in Fujian Province into its risk alert management system. The bank has continuously promoted the construction of environmental risk warning and classification mechanism, and on this basis helped enterprises investigate environmental risks, put forward suggestions for environmental rectification, enhanced the awareness and management ability of enterprises' environmental risk prevention, and taken the environmental and social responsibilities of banks.

China Bohai Bank has formulated "the Bohai Bank credit business environment and the social risk management method", created new tags for "industrial transformation and upgrading, industrial structural adjustment type, the restricted industries, and tags to identify projects with high pollution, high energy consumption, high house prices and outdated systems in the credit risk management system to establish the green financial environment and social risk management system.

HSBC Bank (China), based on the Equator principle Framework, has established a sustainable risk rating system in the management of credit applications to assess the impact of green projects and the ability of customers to manage them, simplify the investigation procedure of the qualified projects, and to enhances service efficiency. The bank has joined Lujiazui City Green liability Investment principles Initiative in 2017, and participated in a number of green finance research activities to actively promote sustainable financial development in China.

Guangxi Beibu Gulf Bank supported the construction of Wind Power Plant in YulinDarong Mountain scenic spot

Forestry

Zhangjiakou City has carried out a series of activities including planting trees, building ecological barriers in Beijing and hosting Green Olympics. Agricultural Development Bank of China has taken these activities as an opportunity and taken advantage of its policy advantages to connect with the provincial forestry bureau and the local government to tailor its financing scheme. The bank has supported key projects in the construction of national reserve forest bases, promoted the government to establish an "anti-risk repayment fund for the construction of reserve forest projects". By the end of 2017, loans issued for the reserve forest project had amounted up to RMB3.33 billion which had been used to help build the ecological environment for the 2022 Winter Olympics Green Olympics.

Bank of Communications has set up a forestry research team to formulate project credit policies by collecting data, regularly monitoring and visiting the major forestry departments. The bank has also vigorously supported the forestation project of the 120 000 mu eucalyptus base in the state-owned Dongmen Forest Farm in Guangxi, and helped build Asia's largest eucalyptus gene pool. By the end of 2017, the balance of the project loans on fixed assets had reached RMB98 million.

Huaxia Bank has included forestry projects such as building forest resources, and forest farming into the scope of green credit support, which has helped the effective development and utilization of forestry resources, local economic growth and ecological environmental protection.

In line with the State Forestry Administration's opinions on the implementation of Forest right Mortgage loan, the city banks, such as Bank of Hangzhou, Guilin Bank, have activated the assets of forestry enterprises through various innovative financing guarantee methods to solve the problem of "financing difficulties", and actively supported forestry development.

Clean Energy

China Merchants Bank has issued RMB48 million loans to support the biomass thermal power plant project in Heilongjiang Qitaihe City. Using corn straw resources to process biomass fuel for power generation and heating, the power plants can produce more than 200 million kilowatt-hours of electricity each year, provide heat to an area of nearly 2 million square meters, save an average of 80 000 tons of standard coal per year, and significantly improve local air quality. The power plant project has provided financial support for the protection of clear water and blue sky.

In line with the national strategy of energy conservation and emission reduction, Bank of Hebei and other city commercial banks have focused on the development and utilization of clean energy and renewable resources, supported major projects such as wind power, photovoltaic power, and refuse power, and continuously increased credit investment in the field of energy conservation and environmental protection. The energy conservation campaign has promoted green economic development.

Huishang Bank has issued green bonds to raise funds to vigorously support the HuaiBei Zhonghu mine geological environment treatment and the Ma'anshan central urban water environment comprehensive treatment project, among which the HuaiBei Zhonghu project has included comprehensive treatment of 36 100 mu of land in the region, which will later, after the treatment, be turned into 24 500 mu of usable land and 11 600 mu of water area with a storage of 69.27 million cubic meters of water. The treatment can effectively improve the local ecological environment.

Jiangxi Bank has pooled a fund with the green finance bond which has issued 350 million loans to the Luxi county government in 2017 in accordance with the regulations in the setout of the funds, helped the government improve the river water environment ecosystem and ensure irrigation and urban water supply security in the water system of Luxi County, effectively promoted the development of "agritainment", orchard sightseeing and other businesses.

Energy Saving buildings

Wuhan production Park of China Construction Bank has installed a comprehensive utilization system of rainwater to provide water for greening irrigation and rinsing in the park, saving about 4 000 cubic meters of water every year. With waste heat recovery technology, the water source heat pump has been used to recover the waste heat from the data machine room and to provide the heat to the park and domestic water heating. It can save about 5 000 cubic meters of natural gas per day compared with 7 × 24 hours heating of ordinary hot water boiler.

Shanghai Pudong Development Bank has actively participated in the "World Bank-Changning District Energy-saving Building and Low-Carbon City Construction Project", and has carried out energy-saving renovation of 150 buildings of more than 20 000 square meters in Changning District. Shanghai Pudong Development Bank has provided financial support for new buildings and existing buildings in the region. By the end of 2017, World Bank Building Energy efficiency loan project had been awarded a competitive quota of USD20 million, with a cumulative withdrawal of USD60 million. The project had been successfully completed.

Product Service Innovation

Agricultural Development Bank of China has issued RMB3 billion of "bond link" green bond, which helped promote the connectivity of China's bond market infrastructure, and the construction of Shanghai International Financial Center and Shanghai Free Trade Port.

Industrial and Commercial Bank of China has launched its first "Belt and Road Initiative" green bond on September 28 2017, actively promoted the concept of China's green development, and served the green "Belt and Road Initiative" construction; the final issuance amounted to USD2.15 billion and received the highest "Deep Green" rating from the International Centre for Climate and Environmental Research and the "Climate Bond" certification of the Climate Bond Initiative.

China Construction Bank has continued to deepen its cooperation with seven carbon trading centers in China to innovate and launch carbon finance credit products. The bank has formulated a "plan for promoting the linkage of carbon finance business with the interbank business", taken the product advantages of "carbon finance" and "central counterparty clearing agent business for carbon quota forward trading", and improved the construction of the green financial product system.

Product Service Innovation

Shanghai Pudong Development Bank has partnered with Asian Development Bank to launch its first green syndicated loan project, which was used by the Green Power and Environmental Protection Group to promote PPP waste generation projects in small and medium-sized cities.

Bank of Beijing has issued RMB30 billion of green financial bonds in 2017 to support energy conservation, pollution prevention, resource conservation and recycling, clean transportation, clean energy, ecological protection and climate change adaptation, and to reduce the cost of green credit financing as well as strengthen green industry support. By the end of 2017, the loan balance of over 70 projects had amounted to nearly RMB16 billion.

Bank of Wenzhou has strengthened cooperation with environmental protection departments to study the characteristics of economic development in the field of energy conservation and environmental protection, and has innovated and developed credit products such as "small hydropower integral asset mortgage", "accounts receivable pledge", "emission right pledge, etc. The bank has promoted the sustainable development of green industry.

(2) Implementing Green and Low Carbon Projects

The banking finance institutions have actively responded to the national call for energy conservation and emission reduction, adhered to the "green development" low-carbon finance "business philosophy", and continued to pay attention to the operational process of resource consumption and environmental impact. The institutions have pushed forward online office system to further reduce paper consumption in offices, vigorously developed online finance so as to constantly enhance the proportion of online financial services through micro, personal consumer credit and credit cards, so that the traditional off-line businesses processing links paper consumption and customer travel costs can be greatly reduced. Banking finance institutions have actively carried out energy-saving, water-saving and oil-saving actions to improve the efficiency of the use and recycling of office supplies, for instance, recycled electronics waste in a safe and environmental-friendly way, integrated environmental assessment into supplier admission standards in centralized procurement links; in the process of centralized purchasing, the banking financial institutions have adopted qualified technology, equipment and materials, created a green office environment; the institutions have also organized a variety of green public welfare activities, such as planting trees, riding and so on, to construct green culture of banks and to enhance employees' awareness of environmental protection.

▶ Banks in Action

China Construction Bank has incorporated the green concept into the procurement management system, set green admittance requirements and evaluation criteria for products and services in the procurement and bidding process, and ensured that the pollution control work of suppliers in the production process meets the relevant requirements, provided efforts to create an inter-industry green management of the ecological environment. A supplier communication meeting was held in 2017, and representatives of 23 key suppliers have been invited to participate in in-depth exchanges and discussions on the effective implementation of environmental and social responsibilities in cooperation on procurement projects.

China Mingsheng Bank has strengthened the centralized management system of purchasing price, quality, supply and service, giving priority to the purchase of recyclable and reusable materials and environmentally friendly marking products with little negative impact on the environment. In the construction and decoration of business and office buildings, adhering to the tenet of "conducting economic and thrifty operation concept," the bank has paid attention to exploring energy consumption and efficiency, ecology and science and technology, integration and optimization, sharing of benefits between present and future, improving the efficiency of building use, and actively building green banks.

贵安集团 中国光大银行贵阳分行 —— 携手创绿 共植未来

China Everbright Bank in Jinniu Lake Park, Gui'an District, launched a tree-planting campaign of "create Green together for the Future"

Bank of Shanghai has strictly controlled the green procurement in terms of selecting suppliers with four selection criteria, including the ratio of suppliers to the use of environmentally friendly materials, the compliance of environmental protection rules, the implementation of ISO14001 clean production and environmental management production mode with upgraded technologies, so as to ensure a green, low-carbon, healthy office environment.

Construction of the green bank, Nanhai financial center of China Guangfa Bank,

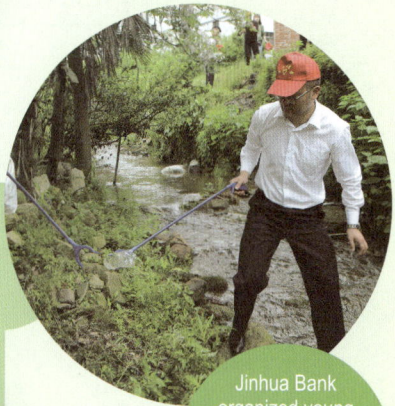

Jinhua Bank organized young staff to join the "Five Water Treatment" River Patrol activities to clean up river refuse

China Cinda Asset Management Company organized green cycling activities, spreading the concept of environmental protection, attracted the participation of more stakeholders, and jointly promoted the protection of the ecological environment

Sumitomo Mitsui Bank (China) held a Wulihe Park walking activities with a theme of "low carbon trip to build a green home"

People-Oriented, Employee Development Strategies

(1) Protecting the Rights and Interests of Employees

(2) Promoting Career Development

(3) Caring the Life of Employees

Harmonious work relationship is beneficial to positive development of enterprises, China's banking financial institutions. Adhering to the concept of being people-oriented, China's banking financial institutions have strengthened the protection for staff's interests, established career development path for staff, conducted all-round and multi-level capability training, launched colorful cultural and sports activities, increased caring for staffs in distress, put in efforts to balance between life and work, exerting great efforts to create optimistic, positive and harmonious working environment for employees.

328 700

employee training programs carried out by banking financial institutions

covered

30.37

million employees

increased by

3.38

million on YoY basis

(1) Protecting the Rights and Interests of Employees

Protecting the rights and interests of employees is the basis for the healthy development of enterprises. Banking financial institutions have strictly abode by and enforced the relevant laws and regulations such as the Labor Law and the Labor contract Law. The institutions have been committed to providing employees with stable jobs, reasonable remuneration and benefits, and to prohibiting the employment of child workers to treating employees of different nationalities, races, genders, religious beliefs and cultural backgrounds fairly and impartially, to providing smooth communication channels and guarantee for employees' basic rights and interests, for instance, the rights to take a break, to take time off and to undergo physical examinations. Banking financial institutions have been committed to creating a respectful, pluralistic and harmonious working atmosphere to enhance the well-being of our employees.

▶ Banks in Action

Jiangsu Bank has opened channel for peer-to-peer communications between all levels of staff, and established employee advice platform. In 2017, the employee advice platform had collected a total of 3 606 recommendations, 3 566 of the total cases were handled, with a coverage rate of 98.9%.

On the basis of the past regular recruitment channels, Beijing Rural Commercial Bank has carried out recruitment for Tibetan college students, retired college soldiers and demobilized military cadres, with a total of 21 people recruited.

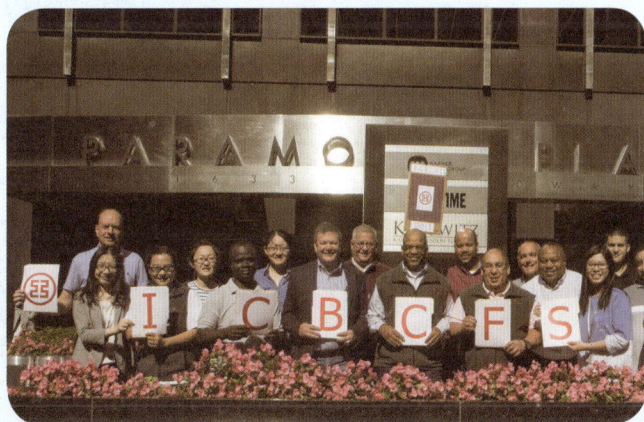

Regional branches of ICBC in US treats employees equally

Guilin Bank held the Fourth Session of the Fourth Workers Congress

---

① Data source: China Banking Association.

(2) Promoting Career Development

Employee career development is an important prerequisite for the sustainable development of enterprises. Banking and financial institutions has continued to strengthen the theoretical knowledge of their staff, attach importance to staff training and personnel training, developed and designed training projects and courses according to the needs of business development and the needs of different levels of staff, carried out employee-tailored training, adopted comprehensive methods of discussion, case studies, video-based training, internet-based training and other ways. The training methods have covered wide topics with appropriate levels, and clear purposes, which created a multi-channel, systematic and all-round training system, and built a 'talent-oriented' employment environment.

▶ Banks in Action

Shanghai Pudong Development Bank has continued to promote the effective transformation of training results to performance results. The bank has focused on interdisciplinary learning and business innovation, explored the development of a curriculum system for innovative development, completed the overall planning framework and the development of sub-framework, in order to create conditions to develop a talent team with cross-disciplinary abilities. The bank has actively introduced case development techniques, focused on summing up practical experience, popularized best practices, improved organizational performance, and combined the construction of training course system and implementation of key training projects. The initial establishment of case development and application management system based on the whole bank management situation has laid a solid foundation for building the internal knowledge sharing platform of Shanghai Pudong Development Bank and accelerating the learning and growth of talents.

China Zheshang Bank has set up an intelligent and mobile/laptop accessible cloud platform with complete functions of learning, testing and training. By the end of 2017, a total of 6 872 employees had participated in the organization of a total of 112 online courses and 26 online tests, with a cumulative duration of 28 555 hours.

A workshop at China Zheshang Bank, where learners and mentors actively interacted with each other.

Bank of Jiangsu organized staff outdoor training

(3) Caring the Life of Employees

Banking financial institutions have continued to care for employees' physical and mental health, balanced their work and life, established and improved staff care systems, strengthened care for female and retired employees, and conducted staff mental health talks, improved the internal mechanism of mutual aid and medical assistance system, provided more helps to the staff in distress, through the development of rich and colorful sports activities to enhance the staff's occupational well-being.

According to incomplete statistics, in 2017[1]

the amount of various assistance funds including disaster relief, medical assistance and livelihood assistance provided by banking financial institutions had reached

RMB
517
million

▶ Banks in Action

In 2017, China Development Bank has carried out multiple kinds of activities, such as psychological testing, telephone counseling and face-to-face counseling, to guarantee the mental health of employees in foreign institutions.

China Bohai Bank has provided a space as the activity center for retirees in the headquarters building, so that the retirees can perform learning activities, acquire the latest information of the market and do exercises. The activity center has met the desire of retirees to carry out life-long learning, and enjoyed the development of the bank.

In order to effectively implement the "Regulations on the Labor Protection of Female Workers of Anhui Province", and to further promote the protection of the basic rights and interests of female workers and care for their work, Huishang Bank has started from the most concerned and basic rights and interests of female employees, actively participated in the discussion of the methods of attendance, held forums for female employees, prepared a lactation room in the head office, set up an interest group of yoga training for female employees, assisted female employees in dealing with family disputes, and safeguarded the rights and interests of the staff of the bank.

In order to further enhance the support of research results to business development, Bank of Qingdao has created a "research results sharing platform" and a "front-line service platform". The theme has included "the study on the sustainable development of commercial banks from the perspective of Green Finance", "the future of banks of China -dual track strategy", "liquidity risk under the marketization of interest rate" and so on.

HSBC Bank (China) has held 10 seminars in Beijing, Shanghai, Guangzhou, Shenzhen and Chengdu, covering various topics such as interpersonal communication, parent-child education and physical education; offered expert hotline consulting. In addition, the multi-inclusive group has organized the staff to practice the Yi Jin Jing, and the health fitness Qigong, maintaining a work-life balance.

Agricultural Development Bank of China held a seminar on employees' mental health

China Merchants Bank held a national relay race

Fudian Bank launched the "Happy Color run" campaign during "International Working Women's Day".

① Data source: China Banking Association.

Devotion to the Public-interest Activities with Passion and Earnestness

Banking financial institutions have adhered to the concept of "responsible banks, harmonious development", pursued the rapid and coordinated development of economic and social interests, practiced the socialist core values, and promoted the public welfare and philanthropy. In 2017, banking financial institutions have continued to improve the public welfare management system, actively promoted the construction of social public welfare projects, and promoted customers to participate in public welfare projects in a diversified manner. Through the establishment of a systematic public welfare management system and long-term public welfare projects, the organizations have effectively fulfilled social responsibility, and contributed our efforts to build a "happy China" and achieve the "Chinese Dream".

RMB
1.04
billion invested in public interests and charity projects

3 307
public interests and charity projects

958 300
hours staff voluntary activities

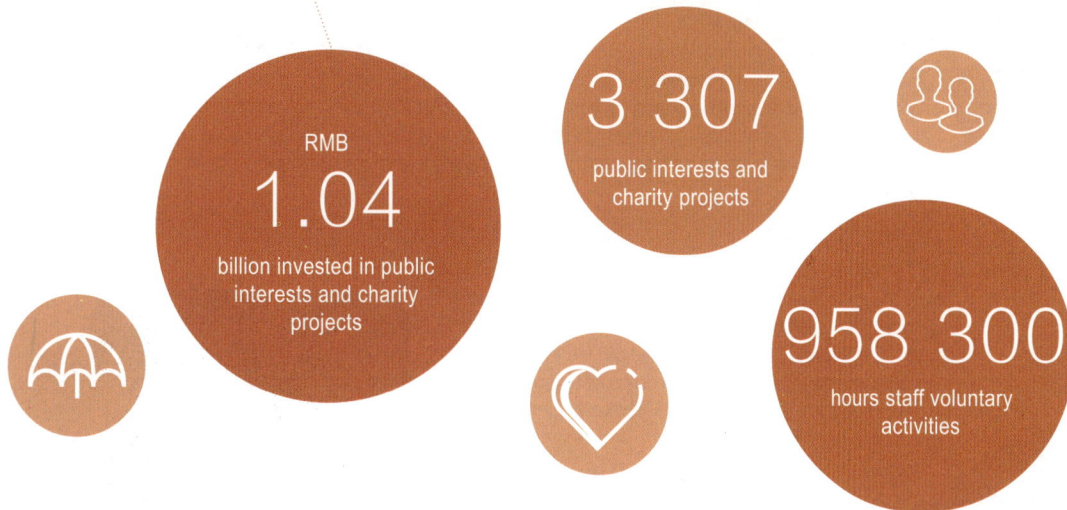

China Development Bank and the policy banks have carried out public welfare projects in the areas of poverty alleviation and assistance to the elderly, such as the "yellow bracelet action" public welfare projects in which China Development Bank participates. The fourth generation yellow bracelet, which has the functions of real-time location, two-way call, SOS one-click call, security fence, historical track query, etc., has been developed to help the elderly who are likely to get lost.

Large commercial banks have made effective use of the collective strength of their employees of global branches to build a public participation platform and carried out activities including caring for the disabled, green environmental protection, donation for education, and education on public welfare, which integrated public action with business development and created a public welfare brand with financial functions. For example, Agricultural Bank of China has continued to carry out "Small points for big dream" public welfare activity, supported hope projects, provided care to 'home-alone' children and supported ecological protection campaigns. The "Mother Health Express" donated by the China Construction Bank has provided villagers with health advice, free consultation, free delivery of pregnant and lying-in women, training of medical workers at the grass-roots level, and special case assistance services in the poor mountainous areas with underdevelopment and inconvenient transportation.

Joint-stock banks, city commercial banks and asset management companies have set up the concept of public welfare during the promotion of the development of public welfare, forming a public welfare charity mechanism. On the basis of the advantage of main business and a well-designed platform, the institutions has set up public welfare funds, public finance, and charitable trust, leading social forces to carry out welfare activities of social assistance, disaster relief, poverty relief, disabled assistance, elderly assistance, and youth assistance.

Joint-stock banks and asset management companies have conducted series of welfare activities with unique features, for example, China Everbright Bank's "Water Cellar Plan", PingAn Bank's "May you be safe throughout the journey. - let love come home", China Guangfa Bank's "Guangfa Hope Charity Fund", China Merchants Bank's "More Pleasure from Monthly Donations", "Little Point and Micro-Philanthropy", Shanghai Pudong Development Bank's "Love and Light Guide Dogs support Program", Industrial Bank's "Beautiful wish to offer Green Love", China Minsheng Bank "Power of Minsheng's Love — ME Charity Innovation Funding Scheme", China Zheshang Bank's "Love into Mountain", China Cinda Asset Management Company's "Caring Love to the Community", Wanxiang Trust Company's "Shanshui Trust Fund".

The city commercial banks have also got involved in public welfare activities. Bank of Chongqing has carried out the activity helping the workers working outside to return home during Spring Festival; Bank of Jiangsu has continued to issue the public welfare financial management product to bring benefits to family member of employees; WeBank has continued to give full play to the advantages of the "good idea" program, so that children in poor areas can have free lunch; Guangxi Beibu Gulf Bank, Panzhihua City Commercial Bank, Bank of Cangzhou and other banks have sustained public welfare activities with volunteer teams.

Rural commercial banks and rural credit cooperatives have also carried out diversified public welfare practice. The rural credit cooperatives in different areas, such as Inner Mongolia Autonomous region, Jiangxi, Hunan, Guangxi Zhuang Autonomous region, Liaoning and Sichuan, have actively promoted volunteer service activities; Chongqing Rural Commercial Bank has carried out intellectual aid activities which bring hope and warmth to the poor students of Shihe Primary School in Shituo Town, Fuling District; Guangzhou Rural Commercial Bank has carried out the "silent love of the sun", an activity that brings hearing-impaired children back to the audible world.

In addition, some foreign banks have support the development of public welfare through the establishment of public welfare funds, the creation of public service brand platform, the development of volunteer services and other practices. Hang Seng Bank (China) has established the "Young Academy of assets and wisdom" to foster the correct concept of wealth among young people and to promote the growth of young people's wealth quotient. Sumitomo Mitsui Bank (China) has launched a "little light to illuminate you and me" charity bazaar, a visiting activity and other activities.

① Data source:Data Collected by China Banking Association.

Escort Plan

The Escort Program is a large national public welfare project initiated by China Children and Teenagers' Fund. It is a new ecosystem which includes a Chinese international student registration system, one-stop service platform and an off-line industrial cluster, providing safeguard to students studying abroad. In 2017, China CITIC Bank has donated RMB10 million to the Escort Program and provided exclusive banking services, cultural identity development services and safety rescue services to underage overseas students in order to make them more cultural consciousness and cultural self-confidence while they are studying at ease.

Block Chain Technology for Charitable Public Welfare

China Everbright Bank has set up block chain public donation system for the "Mother's Cellar" charity project, and realized the disclosure of donation information, the traceability of donation costs, the non-tampering of account information, and the privacy protection of donors which has effectively promoted of transparency of public donations.

Since 2005, China Everbright Bank has been working with All-China Women's Federation and China Women's Development Fund to solve the problem of drinking water and water use for residents in arid and water-scarce areas in the western region. Over the past 13 years, a total of RMB34.33 million has been donated to build 8 593 water cellars and 76 small-scale water conservancy projects in 12 provinces (regions) such as Gansu, Ningxia, Inner Mongolia, Shaanxi, Guangxi, Sichuan, Qinghai, Tibet, Guizhou, Xinjiang, Jilin and Shanxi and 6 campus safe drinking water projects, which has solved drinking water shortage problems for nearly 130 000 people in poor areas.

"Mother's Cellar" charity project launched by China Everbright Bank

"Love and Light" Guide Dogs Support Program

As the public have gained wider awareness of guide dogs, guide dogs have been given access to more places. However, the prevalence of guide dogs in China is far from reaching the 1% penetration rate stipulated by the International Guide Dogs Federation. Training a guide dog takes 2~3 years and costs as much as RMB100 000.

In December 2017, Shanghai Pudong Development Bank has worked with private banks clients to continuously launch public welfare financial management products. A portion of the customer's earnings will be donated to the Dalian Charity Association's "Love and Bright Guide Dogs Support Program", plus Pudong Development Bank have accompanied donation at 1:1 rate. It is estimated that clients will donate RMB375 000 with the product sales of RMB1 billion.

Shanghai Pudong Development Bank launched "Love and Light— Pudong Development Bank Guide Dogs support Program"

Public welfare campaigns of PingAn Bank

PingAn Bank has planned and held nearly 100 kinds of activities of respecting the elderly for four consecutive years in various branches throughout the country. The business outlets have held meaningful activities, such as health lectures and blood pressure measuring for the elderly customers, built voluntary teams walking into the community and care homes to visit the elderly and delivered love and wishes to the elderly. This public welfare activity has not only sent the care and blessing of PingAn Bank to the elderly, but also conveyed the idea of respecting the elderly to the whole society.

PingAn Bank launched the theme activity of respecting the elderly.

Ten Years of Charity, footprint of hope

In 2008, China Guangfa Bank and China Youth Development Foundation have jointly set up the "Guangfa Hope Charity Fund". Over the past 10 years, the bank has worked with all sectors of society to build a charitable public welfare platform to pool social resources and continuously improve the health and educational conditions of young people, passing on positive energy from the charity, through the investment and subsidy in education, poverty alleviation and relief, disease treatment, and so on. Over the past decade, volunteers have spread to the poverty-stricken areas of Shaanxi, Sichuan, Gansu, Qinghai, Xinjiang, Yunnan, Guizhou, Guangxi, Ningxia, Henan and Hubei. By the end of 2017, Guangfa Hope Charity Foundation had had 100 staff volunteers and 50 cardholder volunteers, with more than 10 000 hours of volunteer service, raised RMB75.2 million, directly helped more than 26 000 students and improved the living and learning environment of 150 000 adolescents.

China Construction Bank held "Dream take-off, China Construction Bank Hope Summer Camp" public welfare activities

Young volunteers from Agricultural Bank of China had activities with Home-Alone Children on the Children's day

Staff from Australia and New Zealand Bank (China) visited autistic Children

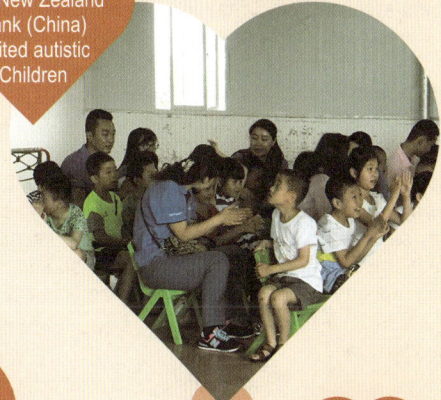

HSBC Bank (China) carried out a service project dispatching volunteer teams to schools

Future Prospects

In 2018, China's banking financial institutions should fully implement the spirit of the 19th CPC National Congress, keep the original aspirations as well as the original mission in mind, fully implement the new development concept of "innovation, coordination, green, openness and sharing", allocate resources and promote development in a coordinated manner. China's banking financial institutions should be committed to "deepening supply-side structural reform, implementing the strategy of rural revitalization, speeding up the improvement of the socialist market economic system", focusing on "serving the real economy, preventing and controlling financial risks," and deepening the reform of the financial system, forging ahead constantly on the road of high-quality development.

Serve the real economy. China's banking financial institutions should stick to their roots, return to their main business, actively adapt to the new normal of economic development, seize new opportunities, actively serve the supply-side structural reform and speed up the construction of "Belt and Road". China's banking financial institutions should also coordinate the development of regional coordination strategies such as "coordinated development between Beijing, Tianjin and Hebei, and the construction of the Xiong'an New area," and constantly enhance the ability to innovate, optimize the credit structure, and devote more credit resources to new industries, advanced manufacturing industries and innovative industries so as to improve the quality and efficiency of economic development.

Committed to inclusive finance. China's banking financial institutions should actively implement the decisions and arrangement made by Party Central Committee and the State Council, vigorously support small and micro enterprises, "agriculture, rural areas," and targeted poverty alleviation and other weak links in economic and social development, and strive to solve the problem of difficult financing and expensive financing as well as speed up innovative product channels, make up for service gaps, use big data, artificial intelligence and cloud computing, accurate customer portrait, expand inclusive financial coverage, constantly improve the quality of financial services, create a new milestone of inclusive financial innovation and development.

Provide convenient services. China's banking financial institutions should take "serving the country, serving the society and serving the masses" as the creed, deepen the construction of the service management system, promote the interconnection between online and offline channels, and adopt the "artificial + intelligent" multi-position service mode. Also, the institutions should promote a new type of customer interaction experience to continuously upgrade financial services to meet the all-round multi-level financial consumption experience and constantly strengthen the protection of consumer rights and interests improve service quality and improve customer experience.

Promote green development. China's banking financial institutions should always adhere to the green development concept that clear water and green mountains are the sources of wealth, constantly establish and perfect the green development system mechanism, develop green finance, and strengthen the energy-saving and environmental protection industries, cleaner production industries and clean energy industries. Moreover, the institutions should strengthen the disclosure of green financial information, speed up the innovation of green financial products and services, solve the problem of harmony and symbiosis between human being and nature, and help the construction of ecological civilization to a new level.

Promote social harmony. China's banking financial institutions should make in-depth efforts to overcome poverty, extensively devote themselves to social welfare and charitable undertakings, enable the people to share the good welfare brought about by economic development, and continuously promote the all-round development of their employees, create a healthy development environment, improve the well-being of the staff, make efforts to resolve the contradiction between the growing needs for better life and uneven inadequate development , provide security for a good life, live and work in peace and contentment.

In 2018, China's banking financial institutions must forge ahead, be bold in reform, and unite more closely around the Party Central Committee, with Comrade Xi Jinping as the core in the decisive stage of building a well-off society in an all-round way. With a high sense of responsibility, a sense of mission, a sense of urgency and firm confidence, China's banking financial institutions should work hard to achieve the great rejuvenation of the Chinese nation and strive for the Chinese Dream.

Appendixes : Mapping of Global Reporting Initiative G4 Indicators

		GENERAL STANDARD DISCLOSURES	
Indicators classification	Ranking	Content	Page
Strategy and analysis	G4-1	Provide a statement from the most senior decision-maker of the organization.	Adopted
	G4-2	Provide a description of key impacts, risks, and opportunities.	Adopted
Organizational profile	G4-3	Report the name of the organization.	Adopted
	G4-4	Report the primary brands, products and services.	Adopted
	G4-6	Report the number of countries where the organization operates, and names of countries where either the organization has significant operations or that are specifically relevant to the sustainability topics covered in the report.	Adopted
	G4-8	Report the markets served (including geographic break down, sectors served, and types of customers and beneficiaries).	Adopted
	G4-9	Report the scale of the organization, including: ·Total number of employees ·Total number of operations ·Net sales (for private sector organizations) or net revenues (for public sector organizations) ·Total capitalization broken down in terms of debt and equity (for private sector organizations) ·Quantity of products or services provided.	Adopted
	G4-10	Report the total number of employees by employment contract and gender.	Not adopted
	G4-13	Report any significant changes during the reporting period regarding the organization's size, structure, ownership, or its supply chain.	Not adopted
	G4-14	Report whether and how the precautionary approach or principle is addressed by the organization.	Adopted
	G4-15	List externally developed economic, environmental and social charters, principles, or other initiatives to which the organization subscribes or which it endorses.	Adopted
	G4-16	List memberships of associations (such as industry associations) and national or international advocacy organizations in which the organization:holds a position on the governance body; participates in projects or committees; provides substantive funding beyond routine membership dues; and views membership as strategic.	Adopted
	G4-17	List all entities included in the organization's consolidated financial statements or equivalent documents.	Not adopted
	G4-18	Explain the process for defining the report content and the Aspect Boundaries.	Not adopted
		Explain how the organization has implemented the Reporting Principles for Defining Report Content.	Not adopted
	G4-19	List all the material Aspects identified in the process for defining report content.	Not adopted
Report profile	G4-28	Reporting period (such as fiscal or calendar year) for information provided.	Adopted
	G4-29	Date of most recent previous report (if any).	Adopted
	G4-30	Reporting cycle (such as annual, biennial).	Adopted
	G4-31	Provide the contact point for questions regarding the report or its contents.	Adopted
	G4-32	Report the "in accordance" option the organization has chosen.	Adopted
		Report the GRI Content Index for the chosen option.	Adopted
		Report the reference to the External Assurance Report, if the report has been externally assured.	Not adopted
	G4-33	Report the organization's policy and current practice with regard to seeking external assurance for the report.	Not adopted
		If not included in the assurance report accompanying the sustainability report, report the scope and basis of any external assurance provided.	Not adopted
		Report the relationship between the organization and the assurance providers.	Not adopted

GENERAL STANDARD DISCLOSURES			
Indicators classification	Ranking	Content	Page
Governance	G4-42	Report the highest governance body's and senior executives' roles in the development, approval, and updating of the organization's purpose, value or mission statements, strategies, policies, and goals related to economic, environmental and social impacts.	Adopted
Ethics and integrity	G4-56	Describe the organization's values, principles, standards and norms of behavior such as codes of conduct and codes of ethics.	Adopted
	G4-57	Report the internal and external mechanisms for seeking advice on ethical and lawful behavior, and matters related to organizational integrity, such as helplines or advice lines.	Adopted

SPECIFIC STANDARD DISCLOSURES			
Indicators classification	Ranking	Content	Page
Economic	G4-EC1	Direct economic value generated and distributed.	Not adopted
	G4-EC2	Financial implications and other risks and opportunities for the organization's activities due to climate change.	Adopted
	G4-EC7	Development and impact of infrastructure investments and services supported.	Adopted
	G4-EC8	Significant indirect economic impacts, including the extent of impacts.	Adopted
Environmental	G4-EN3	Energy consumption within the organization.	Adopted
	G4-EN6	Reduction of energy consumption.	Adopted
	G4-EN8	Total water withdrawal by source.	Not adopted
	G4-EN19	Reduction of greenhouse gas(GHG) emissions.	Adopted
	G4-EN31	Total environmental protection expenditures and investments by type.	Adopted
Employment	G4-LA1	Total number and rates of new employee hires and employee turnover by age group, gender and region.	Not adopted
	G4-LA8	Health and safety topics covered in formal agreements with trade unions.	Adopted
	G4-LA9	Average hours of training per year per employee by gender, and by employee category.	Adopted
	G4-LA10	Programs for skills management and lifelong learning that support the continued employability of employees and assist them in managing career endings.	Adopted
	G4-LA11	Percentage of employees receiving regular performance and career development reviews, by gender and by employee category.	Not adopted
	G4-LA12	Composition of governance bodies and breakdown of employees per employee category according to gender, age group, minority group membership, and other indicators of diversity.	Not adopted
Society	G4-SO1	Percentage of operations with implemented local community engagement, impact assessment, and development programs.	Adopted
	G4-SO4	Communication and training on anti-corruption policies and procedures.	Adopted
	G4-SO6	Total value of political contributions by country and recipient/beneficiary.	Adopted
Product responsibility	G4-PR3	Type of product and service information required by the organization's procedures for product and service information and labeling, and percentage of significant product and service categories subject to such information requirements.	Adopted
	G4-PR5	Results of surveys measuring customer satisfaction.	Not adopted